D1101474

How to Sew

NICKI TRENCH

Bath • New York • Cologne • Melbourne • Delhi
Hong Kong • Shenzhen • Singapore • Amsterdam

This edition published by Parragon Books Ltd in 2015

Parragon
Chartist House
15-17 Trim Street
Bath BA1 1HA, UK
www.parragon.com

ISBN: 978-1-4075-1764-3

Pattern designers: Nicki Trench, Sian Brown, Sally Summerfield,
Camilla Perkins

For Butler and Tanner
Project editor: Julian Flanders
Designer: Carole McDonald
Location and techniques photography: Carole McDonald

Flower illustration istockphoto.com/doodlemachine

Additional photos provided by: page 7 Getty Images; page 8
Cath Kidston; page 9 (left) PA Photos; (right) Getty Images;
page 10 (top) Butterick; (bottom left) courtesy Artisan Workshops;
(bottom right) courtesy SVP Worldwide; page 11 (top left) courtesy
Selvedge magazine.

Thanks to Steve Bane Fabrics for permission to photograph the
selection of their fabrics on page 11.

Printed in China

Contents

Introduction

Sewing was once a skill handed down through the generations from grandmother to mother to daughter. In recent years it is less likely that we live around the corner from our mums or our grannies and with the break-up of local communities, the availability of low-price fashions in the high street and the lack of sewing instruction in schools, this traditional skill has taken a dip in popularity. But now, with the increasing interest in things that are not mass-produced, the revival of traditional crafts and the return to fashion of vintage fabrics, sewing is back, big time.

How To Sew is a step-by-step guide to sewing success. If you have always wanted to learn to sew but have never had the confidence or know-how, this book will guide you through with clear, illustrated instructions and an easy-to-follow techniques section. Once you feel confident enough to try to sew something yourself there are over 20 fantastic projects for you to consider. Each pattern is graded and lists the techniques required to make the item so that you

can choose which project is most suited to your ability. Once you've mastered the various techniques you can move on to the more challenging projects. There are instructions on where to buy all the fabric and equipment that you need to get started. There's a brief history of sewing, a section on the rising popularity of sewing today and how this revival has come about.

We show you how to turn interesting vintage, modern or traditional pieces of fabric into something unique and personal. We demonstrate how to embellish and decorate your fabrics with beads, sequins and embroidery using simple instructions with clear diagrams and photography. This book is mainly for beginners. There are also more challenging projects using zips, sleeves, elastic and gathering. Once you have mastered the basics, the next steps will follow easily.

Sewing your own clothes or accessories gives you and your home an interesting and creative edge above those who haven't braved learning the skill. Who isn't flattered when someone asks where they bought some gorgeous item and they are able to say, 'I made it myself.'

Some of the projects in the book make beautiful personalised gifts for your friends or family at very little cost. If you've ever seen a gorgeous piece of fabric, brought it home and not known what to do with it, *How To Sew* will help you turn it into a masterpiece in a very short space of time. You'll never again have to try and blend into the wallpaper at a party because someone on the other side of the room is wearing the same dress or carrying a bag mass produced in a factory for the high street chains, nor will you look around someone else's lounge to find that they have exactly the same cushions and curtains.

Sewing can be as high or low-tech as you make it. It makes your items unique and it's relaxing and fun. Sewing is the new 'staying in' and will soon become the healthiest addiction you've ever experienced.

The Story of Sewing

Sewing is an ancient craft believed to date back to about 30,000 BC when rough cord was used to join pieces of animal skin or fur together to provide rudimentary protection from the elements. With the advent of cloth the skills developed and people began using a needle and thread to produce stitches that bound pieces of fabric together. The earliest known sewing needles were made from bone. The earliest sewing needles made of iron were discovered in Germany, dating back to the third century BC.

There is an argument about who invented the first sewing machine. Some were invented and patented but didn't get past the model stage. But around 1830 the French tailor, Barthelemy Thimonnier, invented and patented the first practical sewing machine, which was used to produce uniforms for the French army. The arrival of the first machines was taken seriously by the seamstresses and tailors of Europe who spent many hours hand sewing garments and upholstery; and their fears were well founded though it took a little time for the invention of the sewing machine to have its full impact. In the 19th century it was thought that women were too delicate, excitable or even not quite bright enough to operate a sewing machine.

Graded patterns
In the mid 1800s home seamstresses were employed by ladies of high standing who could afford to buy fine quality materials and pay to have them made up into fashionable garments. Those who couldn't afford this luxury would pull existing clothes apart to use as the model for new ones. Sewing patterns, which were graded by size, were first created by Ebeneezer Butterick, an aspiring tailor from Sterling, Massachusetts, in 1863, and almost overnight dressmaking became accessible to people of all classes. Suddenly fashion was in vogue. These graded patterns, first made from thick cardboard but soon replaced by easily foldable tissue paper that could be slotted into envelopes, are still the most popular method of dressmaking at home.

Early sewing machines were hand operated and the electric machine became popular in the 1920s, but it was some time before it replaced the old hand-operated machine.

In more recent history, particularly during the First and Second World Wars, women were encouraged to sew for their country. Clothing factories stopped producing for the domestic market and started making uniforms and parachutes instead. The slogan for women who still had to produce clothes for their families became 'Make Do And Mend'. Like everything else during the war years clothes and materials were hard to come by, as many Merchant Navy ships carrying everything from foodstuffs to domestic fabrics were sunk. This brought about the *Sound of Music* syndrome: making use of whatever fabrics you already had. Quite often, as Julie Andrews did in the famous film, people made dresses and shirts from the fabric that had previously been the drawing room curtains.

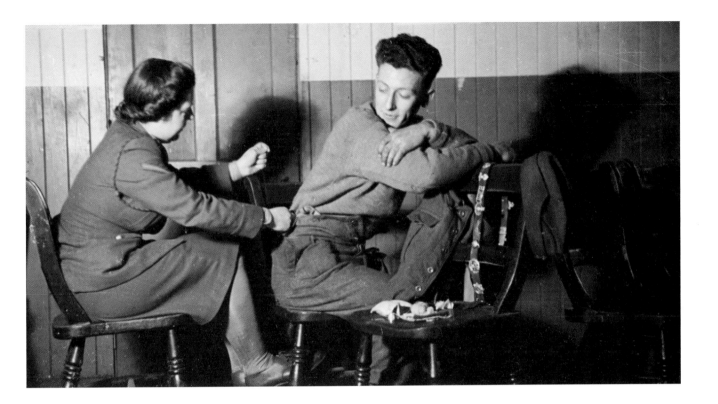

Hobby not necessity

During the 1950s sewing at home went into decline as ready-made clothing became more and more affordable. After the shortages of the war years and the austerity of the post-war period anything home-made was regarded as second best. Those women that still sewed did it as a hobby rather than as a necessity. Sewing classes in schools became less popular with the advent of women's liberation in the 1960s.

Ironically, today it is said that the invention of the sewing machine brought about the liberation of women – because a project that might take seven hours of hand sewing would only take two with a machine, allowing women more leisure time. Eventually the domestic sewing machine was promoted as a timesaver so that women could spend more time taking care of their families. Early machines were incredibly expensive and several families would invariably club together to buy one. Then instalment plans and credit schemes were put into place and more family homes were able to invest in one of their own.

However, although sewing has sometimes gone out of fashion, it has always been a craft that has straddled the boundary between craft and art – a discipline in which necessity has often developed the skills that could produce a thing of real beauty. We've come a long way from garments that gave us simple protection from the elements but we can still gain much satisfaction from a simple yet well-executed piece of work.

Opposite **Hand operated vintage Singer sewing machine.**
Top **Make Do And Mend** – 1943-style.
Above **The Von Trapp family** sporting the newly sewn drawing room curtains in the *Sound of Music.*

Sewing fulfills a basic instinct for creating. It's an addictive pastime which, once mastered, gets you hooked. But during the women's liberation in the 1960s and 1970s sewing became unfashionable and uneconomical as the surge of cheap ready-made garments in the shops turned home sewing into a hobby rather than a necessity. Women were then fighting against the restrictions of the home and rejecting anything home made in a bid to meet the equality of men at work.

Stitched up

In the 1980s and 1990s home crafts took a back seat to shoulder pads and big hair. Women most certainly didn't want to be constrained by the crafts of their grandmothers' day. Busy proving themselves in the workplace and, for the first time, achieving jobs alongside men, they took to spending weekends on team bonding exercises either paint balling or abseiling rather than by the fireside with a needle and thread.

In the 21st century, however, there has been a change in attitudes towards home crafts. Professional women are turning to recreational home craft hobbies again such as sewing, knitting and cooking in an effort to get away from their daytime stresses of hard drives, monitors, CPUs and board meetings. It's not uncommon to find bankers, fund managers and accountants spending their weekends at their sewing machines or at a sewing workshop, creating something wonderful with fabric.

The trend for decorating your own home has filled DIY stores with customers every day of the week for some years. TV programmes and satellite channels dedicated to home decoration have reached epidemic proportions and while the men return home armed with pots of paint, drills or screws, women are either out, or on the internet, searching for fabrics and textiles to colour coordinate their homes with cushions, upholstery, curtains and any amount of accessories.

Inspiring fabrics

With the price of clothing reaching an all-time low, there is always the risk that you'll buy something on the high street and get all excited only to find that your best friend and several others have bought the same garment from the same shop, even though they live in a completely different city. Bespoke and hand-made garments are very costly even if they've just been edged or embellished by hand. So it's no surprise that sewing has risen in popularity in recent times.

Opposite **A** selection of Cath Kidston's 'feelgood' fabrics.
Above Sewing classes in schools became less popular in the 1960s.
Right Sienna Miller attends the 2007 BAFTAs in a vintage-style dress.

Your own hand-sewn garments are unique, they fit you exactly, you can add trimmings that make them totally individual and all for a really great price.

But perhaps the best thing of all is the incredible range of materials and fabrics that is now on the market. Take yourself down to the nearest fabric shop or department store and look at what's on offer. I guarantee you will be inspired when you start to imagine yourself wearing something that you have made for yourself in a fabric and a style of your own choice. It's enough to make you pick up a needle and thread.

Vintage revival

Today, there is a huge trend for vintage-style fabrics. Designers such as Cath Kidston, who has turned pretty vintage florals into contemporary style, have added to the trend for 'feel good' fabrics and wallpapers. Her shops have become so popular in the UK that she's become a household name and has opened shops in New York and Tokyo.

Even the richest and most glamorous Hollywood stars are realising that the classiest look for the red carpet is a vintage dress. Charity shops are being inundated with teenagers and young people seeking out a bargain for a vintage-style piece of fabric or clothing that is unique, which no one else is wearing.

High street chains are opening vintage-style departments selling clothes with pretty prints and florals. Fabric shops are following the vintage fashion too and there is an abundance of beautiful vintage florals, spots and prints lining the shelves.

These inspiring fabrics are particularly appealing to young adults who are seeking out the most trendy fabric shops and prompting a revival in the popularity of sewing. But, faced with the lack of their grandmothers' skills, they're also seeking out places where they can learn how to sew.

Sewing was taught in schools up until the early 1980s when most girls learnt the basics of sewing if these hadn't already been passed down through the family. Education has since changed quite dramatically and the focus is now

Unlike knitting, sewing is usually a solitary hobby. Knitting groups have it easy, they just have to stick their needles and yarn in a bag and off they go. Sewers have a lot more equipment to transport. Just carrying a sewing machine can do your back an injury and you definitely need a table on which to set up the machine. So the Stitch Lounges sound ideal for those who don't like being on their own and they make sewing a far more sociable activity.

Of course, quilting and patchwork are well known for being a communal activity. This is because it's a more portable occupation. Quilts are often hand sewn and quilting circles where women join together to form one big quilt for a particular community have been popular for generations, though machine-sewn quilts are also popular once again.

on more academic courses. This has left the current generation unable to thread a needle or sew on a button so, having bought a mound of fabric, they are then faced with the challenge of making something out of it.

Hip to hem

Thankfully, sewing workshops have sprung up in abundance in the last few years, offering a whole range of classes and now you just have to search the internet to find a course near you. But there are other developments too. In large cities in the US and Europe, such as New York, Los Angeles and Berlin for example, rent-by-the-hour sewing spaces and so-called Stitch Lounges are popping up and creating a lot of interest from all sorts of people. Based on the concept of the internet café, people get together in a room equipped with sewing machines and a big cutting table and sew. Chances are you will find other sewers of your standard, meet a few nice people and it is likely that there will be someone there who can give you a helping hand with any sewing problem you might encounter. These sewing cafes are packed with young people seeking a new skill from an old craft.

Sewing on the comeback trail

With the explosion of popularity for electrical gadgets for the home and personal use such as iPods, mobile phones, palm computers and kitchen equipment, women and some men are adding a new item to their list: a sewing machine. There has been a dramatic rise in the sales of sewing machines. In the US, Singer report that their sales have doubled since 1999, during which time they have recorded five million new sewers. According to the Home Sewing Association, there are approximately 35 million sewing hobbyists in the US, up from about 30 million in 2000. Lucy Wright, the haberdashery and fabric buyer from the John Lewis partnership chain in the UK, reports that John Lewis are expecting the sewing trend to follow from the US. They are opening a further ten stores in the next five years and each will have a fabric department. Their aim is to buy in popular and trendy fabrics to keep up with fashion demand.

Martha Stewart, the guru of home crafts and interiors, has for years been an advocate of all things home made.

Her influence has affected many people worldwide, she has her own TV show *Martha*, she is the author of several books and hundreds of articles on domestic arts and she has just endorsed the Singer, Husqvarna Viking and Pfaff sewing machines.

Sewing and stitching trade shows have increased in the UK; the biggest craft trade show, the Creative Stitches and Hobbycrafts show, has had an approximate 40 per cent increase in attendance over the past four years, indicating that, due to demand, retailers are increasing their sewing and textile departments.

Sewing magazines

This new interest in textiles is also reflected in the number and style of new magazines available. New publications such as *Selvedge*, launched in May 2004, now has a circulation of over 75,000 (40 per cent of its subscribers being in the US) and still rising. Editor Polly Leonard dispels the myth that textiles are something your granny crocheted and uses exquisite photography to bring a visual delight of fabrics, colour and texture with each edition.

There are magazines for sewers of all kinds on the news stand. They are a good resource for learning, often have

tips and lists of workshops and courses available as well as reviewing the new gadgets on the market. They also cover current fashion trends and book reviews and are packed with patterns and information. Some of the more popular titles are: *Burda*, *Sew News*, *Thread*, *Sewing World* and *Sew Today*.

It's not difficult to understand why sewing has never gone away. It is said that 'sewing mends the soul' and it seems that this ability has kept the skills alive. It may sometimes have been brushed to one side, but it has never been forgotten, it has always been bubbling away in the background waiting for its next revival. Sewing evolves to meet each new generation's needs and is a skill that suits all ages and cultures.

A startling example of how sewing has penetrated every walk of life is that it has even found its place in space. A sewing kit was used to repair a blanket on the outside of the space shuttle recently. Astronauts usually take a sewing kit to repair their space suits, and it appears that the duct tape they usually use to secure the blanket on the outside of the shuttle wasn't strong enough so they used stainless steel wire as thread and an instrument with a rounded end that looks like a darning needle to mend the shuttle.

Opposite top **Butterick patterns, still going 143 years after they were first invented.**

Opposite bottom left **Sewing workshops are great places to learn new sewing skills.**

Opposite bottom right **Martha Stewart has endorsed Singer sewing machines and sales have soared.**

Above **Cutting edge publishing from *Selvedge* magazine.**

Right **The range of fabrics available today is nothing short of inspirational.**

Equipment

What you'll need

Listed in this section is the basic equipment you'll need when you're learning to sew. But if you're into gadgets you can find a whole array of interesting pieces on the market.

BOBBINS (1)
Sewing machine bobbins feed the bottom thread of the sewing machine. Follow the instructions specific to your sewing machine to wind thread onto the bobbin and insert into the machine. Always keep several bobbins wound with different shades of thread.

COTTON AND THREAD (2 & 3)
Thread comes in so many colours that you should always be able to match the colour of the fabric you're using. If you are using multi-coloured fabric always choose thread that matches the strongest colour. If you can't find an exact match, choose a darker shade. When in doubt, use white.

It's worth investing in good quality thread. Cheap threads are made from the leftovers of quality threads. They break easily, even when you are hand threading, and leave dust

fibres in your sewing machine that will eventually affect its function. Cotton threads are used on natural fibres. They have a matt appearance and have no flexibility, and are therefore more delicate and break more easily. Polyester threads are more durable and suitable for synthetic fabric or fabric that stretches; they have a slightly shinier finish. You can buy heavy duty or specialist threads, such as jeans thread, that comes in a yellow/gold colour. Quilting threads are made of cotton and have a special finish that slips through all the layers. There are also different threads for embroidery and button sewing.

When starting out, don't get too bogged down by the specialist threads; go for an all-purpose cotton or polyester thread. Thread sizes are by weight; the higher the number the finer the thread.

FASTENERS
Hooks and eyes (4)
These come in a variety of sizes and can be an easier way to fasten a garment or item than using a button.

Snap fasteners/poppers (5)
Also found in a variety of sizes, these are handy little items for closing flaps or fastenings.

NEEDLES
Hand sewing needles (6)
You need a needle that is small enough to go through the fabric without stretching it but with a large enough eye for the thread you're using. General-purpose needles generally come in multi-packs in which you should find what you need. If you buy single-size needles the larger the number on the packet, the smaller the needle.

Sewing machine needles (7) *(see page 16)*

NEEDLE THREADER (8)

Sometimes late nights, sore eyes and overtired sewing hands need a bit of help. There's nothing so frustrating as spending vital minutes licking the end of a soggy piece of thread to try and get it through the eye of a needle. Needle threaders are an essential part of a sewing kit as they take all this pain away.

PINS

There is a wide variety of different pins available and when faced with the choice the inexperienced sewer can find it impossible to choose which ones to use. The best thing is to invest in good quality pins with a reputable brand name. They're easier to push into the fabric and less likely to tear it. The following list should help you determine the right type of pin for your project:

Dressmaking pins (9)

These general-purpose pins are made from steel and come in different lengths.

Plastic-headed or glass pins (10)

Another general-purpose pin, but these ones have colourful heads. They are easily visible and easy to pull out.

Wedding-dress/bridal/lace pins (11)

These are longer than normal pins and are specially made for fine bridal fabrics. But they are good to use with any fine fabrics and cottons and, if you pin horizontally, are less likely to break the needle on the machine.

PIN-CUSHION (12)

There are all different shapes and sizes of pin-cushions. Keep yours near the sewing machine and in your sewing area or you'll end up sticking pins all over yourself, or worse, in your mouth. Never put pins in your mouth.

PINKING SHEARS (13)

These are used for finishing off raw edges to stop fabric from fraying. They have a precise zigzag cutting action, and are easy to use.

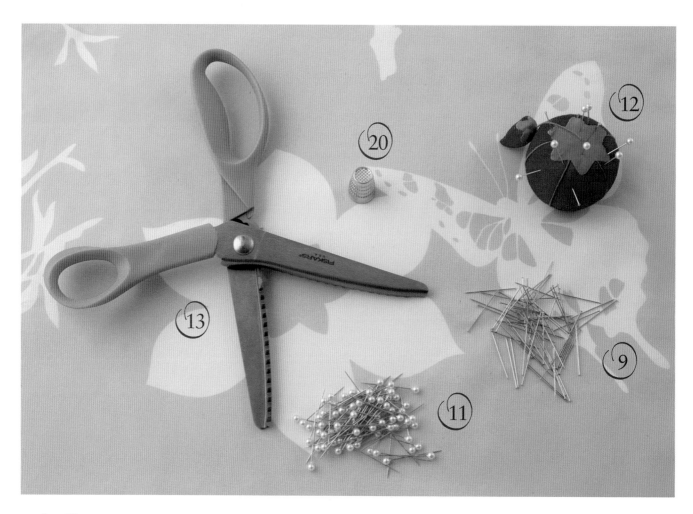

SAFETY PINS (14)
These come in a variety of shapes and sizes and are useful for holding fabrics together or for marking.

SCISSORS (15)
Never use dressmaking scissors for anything other than dressmaking. It's worth labelling the scissors to remind yourself or anyone else in your household that they are for one use only. Most good quality scissors have stainless steel blades and adjustable screws. Dressmaking scissors are approximately 23.5cm (9¼in). They have a flat bottom and a raised handle so that you can rest them on your cutting surface and bring the top cutter down onto the fabric.

SEAM RIPPER (16)
A seam ripper is a tool used for unpicking stitches. It is shaped like a little fork and you slip the sharp blade under the stitches to cut the thread.

SEWING MACHINES (see overleaf)

SEQUINS (17)
These are small shiny discs that reflect light and are used to embellish a garment. They add interest and sparkle to clothes and household items and come in a variety of shapes, colours and sizes.

TAILOR'S CHALK (18)
This is used to mark fabric. There are several types available to buy. The traditional type is made of clay chalk and comes in the shape of a triangle or square. You can also buy wax chalk, but you have to use this carefully because if it is ironed it melts into the plastic. Many chalks are shaped like pencils and are available in different shades so you can choose a colour that can be easily seen on the fabric you are working with.

TAPE MEASURE (19)
Tape measures are made from a ribbon of plastic, metal or cloth. Avoid using a metal one; plastic or cloth measures are better as they bend and curve with your fabric and you can hang them round your neck when you are measuring and cutting. Most measures have metric and imperial measurements on them. This is an essential piece of equipment, something you will use over and over again, so it's worth investing in a good quality tape measure.

THIMBLE (20)
Wear a thimble on the first or middle finger of the hand not holding the needle. It will help you push the needle through the fabric and protect your finger from being pierced.

There are some very sophisticated sewing machines available. There are now computerised machines that you can set to make buttonholes, do complicated embroidery and pretty much everything else as well. But unless you are thinking of sewing professionally, don't waste your time or money on one of these because a basic machine will do the job more than adequately. But do buy from a well-known brand. This will ensure that when your machine needs servicing or you need to buy a particular part, there will be plenty of places to go for help. The major manufacturers are: Singer, Bernina, Janome, Brother, Pfaff, Simplicity and Elna.

Every sewing machine will have its own instruction leaflet and you should follow the instructions that refer to your own specific machine. If you have bought your machine second-hand, look on the manufacturer's website, it will usually give you instructions for your model.

The projects in this book are designed to be simple and are achievable using any machine. You should aim to spend at least £100 on a basic machine. Regard this as an investment. If you keep your machine clean and well oiled it will last a lifetime. Most sewing machine dealers will have displays and will let you try out the machines before buying. Explain that you are a beginner and the sales team should steer you towards an easy-to-use machine that will suit your needs. Look out for a sturdy machine that doesn't wobble. A machine with a metal shell will be more stable and will last longer, although plastic shells are lighter and easier to move around.

Most machines come with different feet. The most basic machines will have a standard foot (1) and a zipper foot (2), More sophisticated machines often have a button sewing

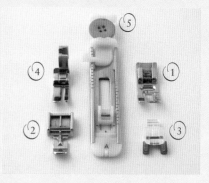

foot (3) and some older machines come with a foot used just for straight stitching (4); this is very good for holding slippery fabric in place. Top of the range machines might have a step button hole foot (5) which adjusts to a selected size. Buy the type of machine that removes the foot with a simple flip lever rather than one that you have to unscrew.

Bobbins are the spools that hold the bottom thread in a stitch. They are tiny things and don't hold that much thread, so you'll end up having to refill them at regular intervals. A good tip is to make sure that the machine you choose has a quick and easy bobbin winder.

When you finally arrive home with your chosen machine practise the stitches and play with the dials. Thread and rethread your machine and wind bobbins. Play with the stitch sizes and make sure you have the correct tension for your fabric. Make sure that you really know your machine before you start making things so that you're not thinking about it when you're sewing. Practise until it becomes second nature; you want your machine to become a sewer's mate.

Before you start sewing, put the machine foot into the down position. Lift it when removing the fabric and make sure the needle is up, otherwise you'll tear the fabric. Before you start sewing wind your bobbin with the colour thread that you're using. If you're sewing a large project, wind several bobbins in advance. Do a test run and stitch a scrap piece of the same fabric that you're using, to check your stitch tension; adjust as necessary.

Sewing machines usually come with a set of needles so you can change them according to your needs. There are many different types for different uses; a general rule is to use finer needles for finer fabrics and thicker needles for heavier fabrics. If your needle breaks during stitching, it may be too fine for the fabric you're using, so try a thicker one. Needles blunt over time, will damage the fibres in your fabric and can cause skipped stitches or puckering. So keep an eye on them and change them regularly.

BUYING A SEWING MACHINE
- Buy a well-known brand
- Try before you buy
- Look for a machine with a needle threader, a zipper foot and with a simple flip lever for changing the foot
- Top loading bobbins are easier and quicker to insert
- Metal shells are more stable and last longer. Plastic shells are lighter and easier to transport
- If you buy mail order, the machine may get damaged en route

Basic sewing machines

All machines will have the basic functions shown on the diagram below. The spool pin is where you place your cotton reel. The bobbin is placed on the bobbin winder which spins the thread from the cotton reel on to the bobbin. The thread on the bobbin is for the underneath stitches and the bobbin sits in the bobbin case. There are some basic dials with numbers and letters on them that indicate the length and type of stitches available on your machine. The plate underneath the needle is called the 'throat plate' and this is where you place your fabric. It has a gap in the middle so that the needle can go through the fabric to catch the bobbin thread below. The balance wheel is for moving the needle manually. Modern machines are multifunctional and can be computerised to do everything except make the tea.

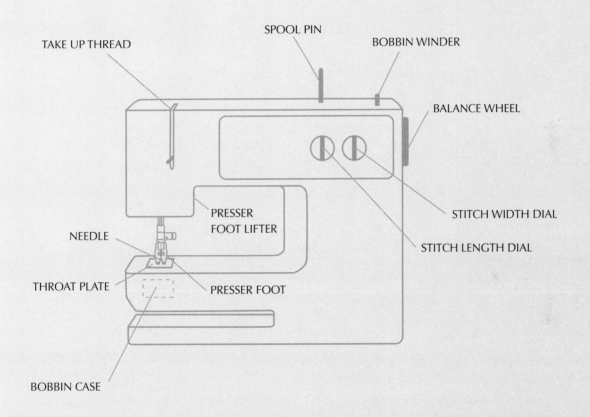

TAKE UP THREAD

SPOOL PIN

BOBBIN WINDER

BALANCE WHEEL

STITCH WIDTH DIAL

STITCH LENGTH DIAL

PRESSER FOOT LIFTER

NEEDLE

THROAT PLATE

PRESSER FOOT

BOBBIN CASE

OVERLOCKER (SERGER)

An overlocker is a machine that cuts and sews a seam or hem as it is fed through the machine and so stops the edges from fraying. It uses four spools of thread at the same time. Overlockers use less fabric because there is no need to allow extra fabric for hems or seams. They can also be used for decorating edges with contrasting colour threads. The method makes the material lie flatter, doesn't give a ridge, and gives your hem or seam a professional finish. Overlockers are becoming hugely popular among home sewers. Once you have moved on from beginner level and have fully committed yourself to sewing, an overlocker can be a fabulous investment. They can cost anything from £200 and over £1,000.

Adding creative embellishments to garments or home accessories gives a professional and individual finished look. The trimmings can often be simple but can make a big statement in the project.

APPLIQUÉ
This is a decoration or trimming cut from one piece of fabric and stitched to another (see the make-up bag on page 80 and the techniques section page 29).

BEADS AND SEQUINS
These are usually sewn by hand. They are cheap and easy to buy and come in a huge range of colours and sizes. They can really glam up a very simple piece of fabric (see the sarong on page 59).

BIAS BINDING
This is a strip of fabric that is cut on the bias of the fabric. It is stretchy and is used to strengthen edges and fit neatly around curves. Bias binding can be bought in different qualities. It has double folds that are sewn around the edge of the fabric (see page 24 in the techniques section). If you put bias binding on the edge of the fabric in a contrasting colour it gives a neat and attractive look to an edge.

EDGINGS AND TRIMMINGS
These can be very decorative but can also be used to cover up raw edges. They can be applied either by hand or on the machine. You can buy beaded, embroidered and tasselled trims. These work particularly well on the edges of curtains.

RIBBONS
Are usually used to decorate and adorn fabrics either as bows, edgings or ruffles (see page 29).

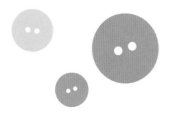

There are all sorts of containers that you can store your tools in. Sewing baskets are widely available and have all sorts of little sections for pins, needles and threads. Even though you start off with one sewing basket you'll soon find the need to expand your stash. Jam jars with lids and plastic stackable containers make brilliant containers.

However, look out at junk shops and markets for pretty boxes and containers because fabrics stored in old-fashioned, characterful suitcases look even better than those in plastic boxes. If you have the luxury of a large linen cupboard then why not display your fabrics and colourful threads in baskets and wooden boxes? You can make a feature of the colours and textiles rather than making your sewing gear look like a messy jumble of old clothes and needles.

Techniques

Before you start

The idea of sewing something that you are going to wear or use around the house can be a daunting prospect, but once you have mastered the simple techniques included in this section you will been able to make your own garments and accessories and a huge world of possibilities will open up for you.

We've kept to the very basics in this section but we have included all the techniques that you need for the patterns featured later. The first hurdles to get over are to know how much fabric to buy, tips for cutting and to learn basic machine stitches. Hemming is used on most projects and putting in a zip correctly can make an amateur project turn into a masterpiece. We show you how to make a seam, make a drawstring waist, explain an easy way to thread elastic and to gather. Pretty linings can make a big difference to a simple tote bag or garment.

Each technique is explained using easy to follow, step-by-step instructions with clear photographs to help you with the simple yet stylish projects we've selected.

THE IDEAL PLACE TO SEW

The first thing to do is create a comfortable place to work. Most people sew on the kitchen table. Cutting out is best done here but make sure that the table is cleared, cleaned and dry. If the fabric is too large you can use the floor but make sure you give it a good vacuum beforehand so your fabric doesn't get covered in bits of grit, pet hair or anything else lurking there.

Get organised and make sure that all your sewing tools are nearby. Keep the ironing board and iron near the area where you're sewing so that you can conveniently press your seams without dragging your fabric from room to room.

Make sure you have good lighting. Sewing is an intricate business so if your overhead light is too dull, change the light bulb or hook up a good anglepoise lamp on the table.

Daylight is the best light for sewing and there are lots of white light bulbs on the market that simulate daylight. These don't distort the actual colour of the fabric and help you avoid eye strain.

Your machine will have its own light that will come on automatically when you switch on the machine, so you can see the stitches.

PATTERN TEMPLATES

Most of the pattern templates in this book are 25 per cent of the actual size so you will need to find a photocopier or printer that can blow up the images by 400 per cent. Find your size on the pattern and follow the instructions. Many fabrics don't have a right or wrong side so it's not easy to tell which is which; a good way to mark the right or wrong side is by putting little coloured sticky dots onto the right side of the fabric. This will help when the instructions ask you to put right side to right side or wrong side to wrong side.

Basic Techniques

MEASURING

Always use a good quality tape measure. Most tape measures are plastic and pliable; usually one side is in feet and inches, the other in metres and centimetres. Choose your preferred system and stick to it – do not mix imperial and metric. Never use your first measurements, always measure twice.

CUTTING FABRIC
(Raw edges and selvedges)

All sewers should live by the phrase 'think twice, cut once'. When you've brought home a beautiful piece of fabric that cost an arm and a leg, you don't want to go ruining it by being scissor happy and making a mistake you'll live to regret.

Using a pair of sharp scissors is essential. Do not use them for anything else apart from cutting fabric as other materials will blunt your scissors.

Hide them and name tag them so that everybody in the house knows that they are yours. Most scissors are made for right-handed people, so if you're left-handed find a specialist shop and buy left-handed scissors.

Lightly iron out any creases in the fabric before cutting. Lay it out on a flat surface. Find as big an area as possible – don't forget that the floor will do.

If you're cutting from a pattern make sure that the pins are well inside the cutting line because if you cut a pin it will blunt your scissors. If you're not using a pattern, draw a line with tailor's chalk or follow the grain or pattern of the fabric to keep your line straight.

Use pinking shears for finishing off seams or anything that might fray, as an easy way to stop the material unravelling. Cut slowly and carefully. Concentrate on getting a straight line.

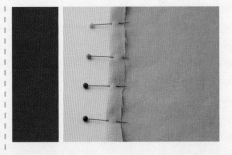

PINNING

When pinning, if possible insert pins horizontally. As you machine, this enables you to sew over the top of the pins without damaging the needle of the machine.

There's a wide variety of pins available but it's worthwhile investing in good quality pins; they're easier to push into the fabric, and they won't tear it. Cheap pins will rust if your house is humid or if you get a splash of tea on them. Use wedding-dress pins if you are using fine fabrics or cottons. Multi-coloured, glass-headed pins are very useful as they're easier to find and less fiddly to pull out.

TACKING

Tacking is the traditional technique used to hold the fabric together after pinning and before sewing. Tacking should be sufficient to ensure that your material is joined together in the correct place, however, pinning and tacking is doubly secure. Use big hand stitches and thread of a contrasting colour to your fabric.

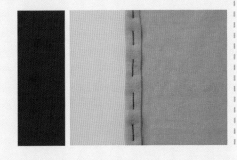

SEWING MACHINE STITCHES
Straight stitch (pic 1)

This is the most commonly used stitch. There are usually 11–12 stitches per centimetre (28–30 stitches per inch). You can set your machine to change the length of the stitches. A longer stitch is usually used for thicker fabrics, or fabrics that have a stretch in them. Also use a longer stitch for fleece fabrics as this stops the fabric puckering or the thread from breaking. Shorter stitches are better for sheer or lightweight fabrics.

Zigzag stitch (pic 2)

You can change the length of the zigzag so the stitches are either close together or far apart. For stretch fabrics such as jersey or T-shirt fabrics use a small zigzag stitch. Some machines have stretch stitches, which allow the seams to flex as necessary without breaking the thread.

When you have finished sewing and you've cut your thread, tie a double knot in the ends and cut.

(For more information on sewing machines see pages 16–17.)

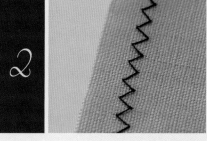

SEAMS

A seam is the line at which two pieces of fabric are stitched together. Most seams in this book are 1.5cm ($^5/_8$in) and this is already allowed for in the patterns.

To make a seam, pin the fabric in place, right sides together. Place it in the machine 1.5cm ($^5/_8$in) from the edge of the fabric. Most machines will have a marker plate to the right of the machine foot (pic 1).

Place the upper and lower threads to the back of the machine.

Lower the foot. Sew straight, following the pattern line to the end (pic 2).

Finish the seam by reversing back over approx 4–5 stitches, stitch forward again to the end (pic 3).

Alternatively, stitch to the end and cut the thread allowing at least 15.2cm (6in); pull one stitch from the front through to the back so that both threads are on the same side (pic 4) and tie in a knot (pic 5).

If you are finishing your seam with a zigzag stitch see Zigzag stitching (opposite).

Always iron seam flaps open. If crossing one seam with another, ensure that the flaps of the first seam are flattened out before sewing second seam.

FINISHING EDGES AND SEAMS

An edge usually needs to be finished to prevent it from fraying.

Raw edge (pic 1)

A raw edge is unfinished and can unravel. Finish raw edges by folding the fabric 0.6cm (¼in), press and then fold another 0.6cm (¼in), pin and sew.

Selvedge (pic 2)

A selvedge doesn't need double hemming or finishing because it's already finished and doesn't fray. This is the woven edge of the fabric that sometimes has the manufacturers details printed on it. However, for neatness, finish the selvedge by folding fabric 0.6cm (¼in), pin and sew. Some selvedges are wide and are better cut off and the edges finished in the normal way. Be careful when cutting out on a selvedge because it may not be the correct width allowance.

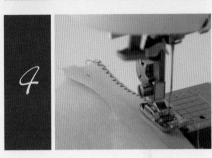

Pinking Shears (pic 3)

Another way of finishing an edge to stop it from fraying is by cutting along the raw edge of the fabric with pinking shears. Cut with pinking shears after sewing your seams.

Zigzag stitching (pic 4)

Before sewing your seams, take a piece of fabric and set your machine to zigzag stitching and stitch along all raw edges.

(When sewing you can use any of the above as your chosen method.)

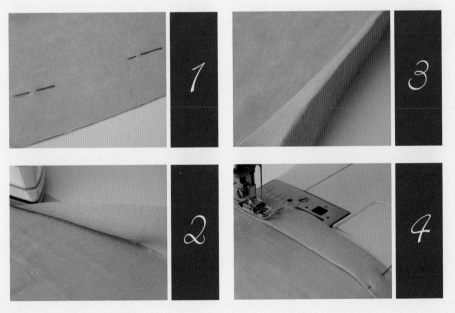

HEMMING

Always press the fabric before hemming.

Make sure the edge of the fabric is straight.

Mark along the edge with marker pins the size of the hem needed (pic 1). (Do not use pins with plastic heads here, the iron will melt them.) For an average hem, measure 1.5cm (⅝in) or measure a bigger or smaller hem as required.

Fold and press at pin line (pic 2).

Remove the pins and open out.

Fold the edge of the fabric to the crease mark and fold over again, press (pic 3).

Pin and sew near the open edge (pic 4).

Finish off by either reverse stitching or tying the loose threads.

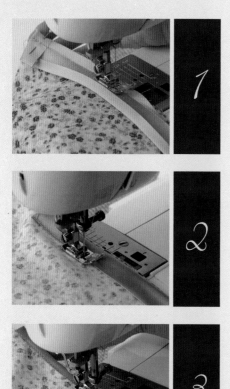

BIAS BINDING

A more advanced and neater way of finishing off an edge is to use bias binding. This is a width of material cut on the cross of the fabric so that it stretches and gives. It strengthens the edge and flattens the seams. You can buy it in different fabrics, colours and widths. It can also be used as a ribbon or, when sewn together, can be used as a tie for a dressing gown or top.

To use bias binding so that it does not show on the outside, open up one side of the binding, place the edge of the bias binding onto the edge of the fabric, right sides together, and place one pin at the start. Sew along the crease of the binding (pic 1). Fold the binding over so that it is not showing and flatten it onto the fabric without opening out the edge. Sew down the the bias binding on the wrong side of the fabric (the right side of the bias binding) (pic 2).

If, however, you want the bias binding to show on the outside of the fabric,

open up one side of the binding, and as before, place the edge of the bias binding onto the edge of the fabric, right sides together, and place one pin at the start. Sew along the crease of the binding (pic 1). Fold the binding in half over the edge of the fabric and sew the binding to itself down the edge on wrong side of fabric (pic 3).

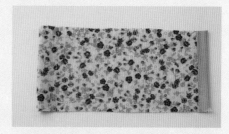

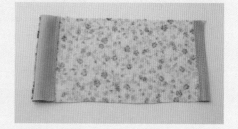

CORNERS

To achieve a neat corner, stitch along the seam in the usual way, then leave the needle in the material, lift the foot, turn the material 90 degrees, lower the foot and continue. When you have finished, cut the excess fabric diagonally across the corner outside the stitching. This neatens the piece when turned the right way out so that it's not bulky and doesn't leave a mark when ironed.

WAISTBAND CASING

This forms a channel so that you can fit a tie or elastic into the waistband.

Measure and mark 5cm (2in) down from the waist edge. Fold along marked line and press. Open out, remove pins. Fold the edge to the crease line. Fold from the crease line and pin, tucking any raw edges under and press again. Sew as near to the bottom edge of the waistband as possible.

CLIPPING SEAMS

When you have a shape in which you need more give, for example the inside seams of trousers or sleeves, you will need to clip the seams as shown to allow the fabric room to move (pics 1 & 2). Take care not to clip through the stitches with scissors.

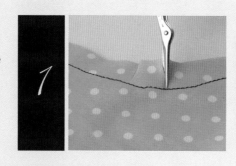

GATHERING

Gathering creates fullness by bunching fabric together. It also allows a longer piece of fabric to be sewn onto a shorter piece. Adjust the machine stitch to the longest length, securing the thread at the beginning. Stitch along to the end of the line that needs to be gathered, leaving a long thread end. Taking the end of the top thread, gather equally, easing the fabric very gently to prevent the thread from breaking (pic 1).

Pull the thread to the required length and then knot together to secure in place. Take the long thread that you've been using to gather. Thread with a hand-sewing needle and hand sew in

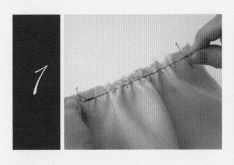
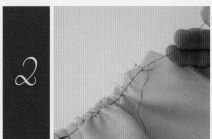

place at the end to prevent the gathers from coming undone. Alternatively bring the thread through from the other side and knot in place to secure (pic 2). When attaching the gathered fabric to the straight piece, always sew the gathered piece on top (pic 3).

PATTERN REPEATS

You may have bought a fabric that has a printed or woven pattern repeated across it. When buying this type of fabric make sure you buy enough so that you can match up the repeated patterns. For example, when cutting out two fronts of a garment, match up the print or weave so that the pattern is at the same place on each side.

LINING

Linings are used to give a garment a more professional finish; they make a garment more comfortable and they add weight, making it hang well. Lining on curtains adds body and stops the light shining through. Use different colour fabrics for linings on bags and purses to give a decorative effect and hide the inside seams and stitching. (See the reversible shopping bag on page 48.)

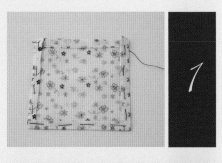
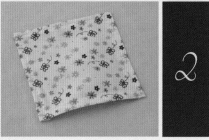

PATCH POCKETS

Patch pockets are both functional and decorative.

For a basic patch pocket cut the pocket to size, hem the top of the pocket and press. Fold the fabric with a 1cm (³/₈in) hem and pin and tack the other three sides (pic 1). Press. Place the pocket on the garment by pinning it in position and sew the two sides and the bottom, leaving the top open. Remove the tacking stitches and press (pic 2). The top pocket corners can take a lot of strain, so it's a good idea to reinforce them by stitching at the top corner, then sew down for 1cm (³/₈in), then sew up and across the top diagonally (*right*).

(See the apron on page 34 and the men's shorts on page 60 for instructions on how to attach a patch pocket.)

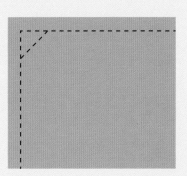

ZIPS

There are many different types, colours and lengths of zip. It is important to buy the right one for the item you are making. If the zip is going to show then you should match the colour or choose another complimentary colour. You can buy lightweight, plastic or heavier zips made from metal. Make sure you buy the type of zip suitable for the weight of the fabric you're using. If you're inserting a concealed zip, the colour is less important, although it's best to buy one that matches the fabric in case it shows a little. If you can't find the exact length you need, zips are available to buy on the roll so that you can cut them to size. They come with a zipper glider that you attach to the zip. Simply stitch at the base of these zips to seal them and stop the glider from falling off the end.

When inserting a zip, if possible use a zipper foot. This has a single toe rather than two toes found on the standard foot of the machine. The zipper foot sits over the left or right of the needle so that it doesn't run over the zip teeth.

How to insert a concealed zip

Put the right sides of your fabric together and measure and pin 1.5cm (⁵/₈in) down along one edge in three places (pic 1).

Place the fabric on the ironing board and fold down one side to the line of pins, press along to make a 1.5cm (⁵/₈in) seam (pic 2).

Fold the fabric and repeat on the other side (pic 3).

Lift up the flaps and tack both sides together along the pressed seam (pic 4). Remove pins.

Open out the seam and press (pic 5).

Place the zip onto the opened out seam and centralise on the fabric, putting a chalk mark or a pin marker on the fabric at each end of the zip (at the end of the teeth not on its flaps).

Take the zip away from the fabric (pic 6).

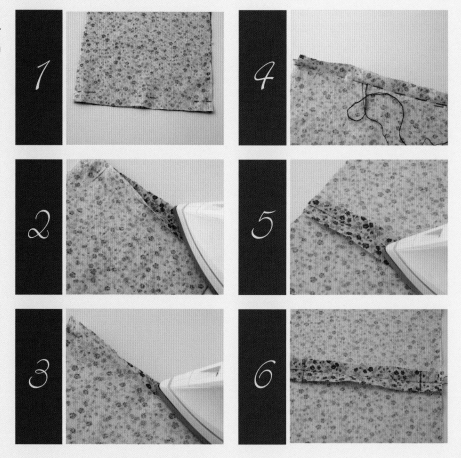

Mark the same point on the wrong side of the flaps (pic 7). With the right sides of the flaps together, sew a short seam at one end of the fabric from the edge of the pressed line to approximately 0.6cm (¹/₄in) past your mark. Repeat at the other end (pic 8).

Remove any pins before pressing. Take the fabric to the ironing board and with the right sides face down, open the seam and press (pic 9).

Place the zip upside down on the seam and centralise again.

Pin and tack the zip in place on the wrong side of the fabric (right side of flaps) (pic 10).

Remove pins from the fabric.

Turn the fabric over and, with the right side facing, take out the middle seam line tacking stitches for approximately three quarters of the length of the zip at the zip pull end (pic 11).

Open the zip approximately three quarters of its length.

Change the foot on your sewing machine for a zipper foot (if you have one). With the right side facing, place the fabric in the machine with the zip horizontal at point A (see diagram right) and sew across at the top of the zip to keep it in place (B). Make sure you avoid the teeth of the zip.

Lift the foot, making sure the needle is down, and turn the zip 90 degrees clockwise. Put the foot in the down position and sew up to the zip puller without the foot coming into contact with it. Keeping the needle in the down position, lift up the foot and close the zip. Put the foot down and continue sewing to the end of the zip (C).

Leaving the needle in the down position, lift the foot and turn the zip 90 degrees clockwise, place the foot down and sew across to the other side of the zip (D) making sure the needle is down when you reach the end.

With the needle down, lift the foot and turn the zip 90 degrees clockwise. Open the zip halfway, put the foot down and sew up to just before the zip pull.

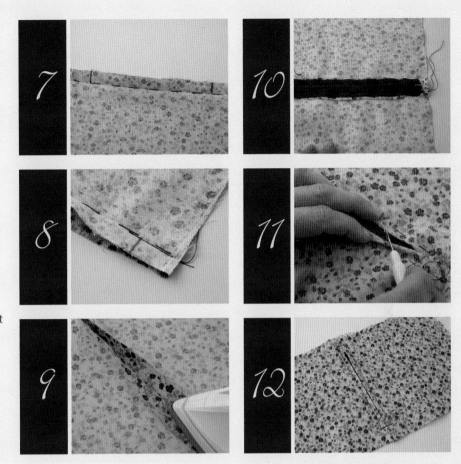

With the needle down, lift up the foot, open the zip further and take down past the foot, put the foot down again and continue sewing to the end of the zip (A). Finish off, cut the thread and take out all the remaining tacking stitches (pic 12).

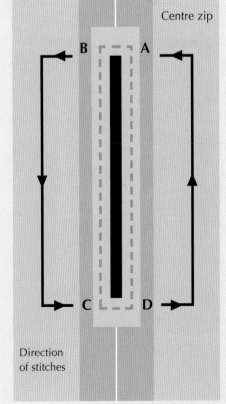

Centre zip

Direction of stitches

ELASTIC
Putting in elastic
You need to make a channel to be able to insert elastic. Either fold down a seam and sew a straight stitch, leaving enough space for the width of elastic needed, or sew a channel of two rows of straight stitch (pic 1). To insert the elastic, either thread the elastic in a bodkin needle (a needle with a very large eye) and feed through the channel, or pin the elastic with a safety pin and feed it through (pic 2). Pin both ends of the elastic in place and stitch backwards and forwards over the elastic at each end to secure it in place (pic 3). This is the same method as waistband casing (see page 24). (See the suntop and sundress on pages 38–41 for garments with elastic.)

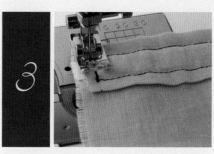

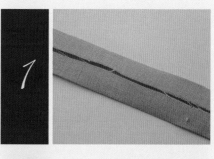

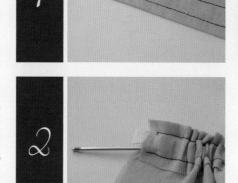

Top stitching elastic
When top stitching elastic and not inserting into a channel, pin the elastic into place along the length of the fabric in small sections at a time. Sew a holding stitch to keep the elastic in place at the start. Stitch elastic in place, stretching it to fit the fabric as you sew.

Use a machine needle with a sharp point, as this will pierce the elastic more easily.

MAKING TIES
Cut pieces of fabric for ties or straps to the length required. Fold each piece in half lengthways and press, open out flat and fold both long raw edges to the centre line (pic 1), fold in half again (you should now have four thicknesses), press and sew along the open edge (pic 2). If an end of tie is going to be on show and not incorporated into a seam, tuck in the raw edge before folding the long edge lengthways.

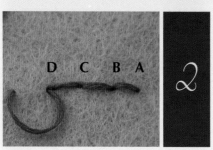

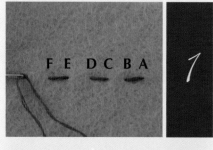

SIMPLE EMBROIDERY
Embroidery adds a decorative finish to your sewing. Many hand embroidery stitches only use basic sewing skills.

Running stitch (pic 1)
Bring the needle up through A, put it down through B, come up again at C, go down at D and come up again through E and down through F. Sew loosely to prevent the stitches from puckering fabric.

Backstitch (pic 2)
Bring the needle up through A. Insert the needle at B and come back up at C and pull thread through. Insert the needle again at B and come up at D. Continue using the same steps.

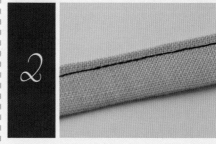

APPLIQUÉ

This is a method of sewing a smaller piece of fabric on top of a larger piece. It's used as a decoration for any garment or accessory and can be sewn either by hand or machine. Modern machines have many different decorative stitches available. For hand appliqué use either a running stitch (pic 1) or any hand stitching for a decorative effect (pic 2).

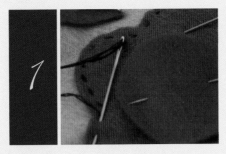

EMBELLISHMENTS

It's easy and effective to personalise a piece of fabric by adding an embellishment such as embroidery, sequins or beads (see the sarong on page 59). Ribbons can also be used for embellishments. They are available in a variety of widths and lengths and the edges are already finished so they don't fray.

Ribbon

Pin the ribbon to the fabric and sew, using a straight stitch, or a zigzag stitch for a more decorative effect (pic 1). You can easily ruffle a ribbon by running a straight stitch along the centre of the ribbon. Secure the threads in place at one end and pull one of the threads to gather up the ribbon. Pin and sew in place (pic 2).

Lace or trimming

Cut the lace or trimming to the required length and pin in place. Stitch in place using a straight stitch.

Beads and sequins

Place a bead or sequin on the right side of the fabric. One stitch through the hole of a sequin is enough to keep it in place, however you may have to sew two or three stitches to keep it flat and more secure. Insert the needle from the back of the fabric and through the hole, stitch over the sequin or bead and stitch through to the back. Tie off at the back of the fabric (pic 1).

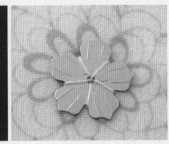

PRESSING

Your motto should be: 'Press, press and press again'. Keep the iron and ironing board near you when you're sewing. A pressed seam can be a very handy stitch line. Experienced sewers sometimes use their press line rather than pinning or tacking.

Always press seams after sewing as this will keep your seams flat and neat.

Before you cut out and start sewing, press your fabric so there are no kinks or creases. Keep the iron in the lengthwise direction of the fabric grain.

Always use a press cloth (unless you are using cotton or linen). This will prevent your fabric from overheating.

Always press on the wrong side of the fabric to prevent a shine from the heat of the iron.

Place the iron gently. Don't press too hard or drag the iron.

Patterns

Before you choose which project to start on, flick through the following section and choose something you like. The patterns are graded in order of difficulty, those marked with one cotton reel are easy while those with two or three reels are a little more complicated. But don't be put off by the three reel projects as they are all aimed at beginners; the methods have been chosen for their simplicity and there are step-by-step photographs to help you through the more complicated pieces.

When you have chosen your project, check the list of techniques used and look them up in the techniques section before you start. Most of the templates are 25 per cent smaller and will need to be enlarged to 400 per cent before you use them, except for the make-up bag, shopping bag, skinny belt or scarf. The tablecloth template is a guide and is not actual size. The slouch trousers for both men and women are 20 per cent smaller and these will need to be enlarged to 500 per cent before you use them. Either take your template to a copy shop and ask them to enlarge it, or use your own printer or scanner and tape the pieces together. Once enlarged, place the template on the fabric and cut out. Where there is a fold, this means that the fabric needs to be folded before the template is placed onto it.

All fabrics are woven and have soft lines – these are called the 'grain'. Always place templates on the grain of the fabric. Place templates as directed, use the arrows as a guide to line up with the grain of the fabric. This is usually parallel to the selvedge.

As a beginner you need easy fabric to work with. I recommend cotton, which we've used for most of the garments in the photographs. Don't choose fabrics that slip around such as silks or jerseys, or fabrics that have naps such as velvets. If your fabric has a pattern and it needs matching, you may need to buy extra material to allow for this. As a general guide you need to measure your pattern repeat and add this amount to the length or width of fabric required (see the techniques section on pattern repeats on page 25).

Always press seams after sewing each section and finish your edges with either a zigzag stitch or pinking shears.

When you are pinning keep the pins on the upper layer of the fabric so they don't get caught in the machine foot. In nearly all our methods we have sewn straight onto pins without tacking. If you don't feel confident enough to sew over pins – pin, tack and then sew.

We've used contrasting thread in the photographs in order to display the stitches. However, you should use a matching colour for your projects. Buy a stash of threads in as many colours as possible and wind them onto your bobbins in advance so that you don't waste valuable time in the middle of a project fiddling with your threads.

When using bias bindings or trimmings don't cut the lengths until you have finished sewing in case of any mistakes in your measurements. Pin them in place first to ensure the binding or trimming is the correct length.

Now all you need to do is choose one of our fabulous designs and follow the instructions to turn you into an overnight expert.

Bunting is a brilliant way to use up spare bits of fabric. This bunting is made using recycled sari fabric in beautiful bright coloured silks. It's the perfect decoration for a summer party in the garden or in the home to brighten up a winter's day.

Techniques used
Hemming (page 23)

CUT SIZES	FINISHED MEASUREMENTS
Fabric	
28.5cm (11¼in) long × 22.5cm (8¾in) at widest point (cut as shown opposite to get the most out of the fabric)	27cm (10¾in) long × 20.5cm (8in) at widest point

115cm (45in wide)

150cm (60in wide)

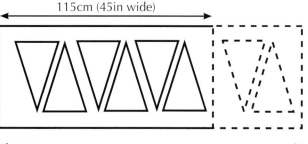

METHOD

1. Pin the pattern piece to your fabric and cut out as many pieces as you want for your bunting.
2. Press a 1.5cm (⅝in) hem on all three sides. Sew using a zigzag stitch (see the techniques section on hemming page 23). When sewing at an angle always line the fabric up with the sewing guideline on the throat plates on your sewing machine. This way you will keep your stitching in a straight line.
3. Press again.
4. Sew the top of each piece of bunting directly onto some tape, lining up each flag 6.5cm (2½in) apart (pic 1).

Template on page 82

A piece of fabric covering a space keeps kitchen shelves cleaner and looking more attractive. You can use this very easy method for any space using a piece of sprung wire tucked into the top of the fabric and just a couple of little hooks and rings. You can either make one curtain to cover your space, or cut the fabric in half to make two small curtains.

Techniques used
Hemming (page 23)

MATERIALS TO BUY
Fabric:
Width: measure the opening and double the width. This allows enough fabric for the gathers and hemming the side edges.
Length: measure the opening and add at least 10cm (4in) extra to allow for the turnover at the top for the wire to slip through and the hem at the bottom.

Small hooks and eyes: x 2 of each
Plastic covered stretch wire: buy 5cm (2in) less than the width space, to allow for tautness.

CUT SIZES

Fabric

Cut as per instruction above, allowing 2cm (¾in) for hems at the sides, 4cm (1½in) for the top and 5cm (2in) for the bottom hem.

TIP
When buying fabric buy double the width to allow for gathers and at least 10cm (4in) for hems and if there is a pattern print on the fabric, allow enough fabric to match up the pattern when cutting (see techniques section on pattern repeats page 25).

METHOD
1. Decide whether you want one or two curtains. Cut your fabric to the correct size. If you want two curtains, then cut the fabric in half lengthways.
2. If you are making one curtain, stitch the side edges by folding the fabric 1cm (³⁄₈in) and press, then fold over another 1cm (³⁄₈in), pin and sew.
3. For the top, fold and press 1cm (³⁄₈in) across the width of the fabric. Fold again 2.5cm (1in), pin and sew stitching as close to the bottom edge as possible, while leaving enough space for the wire to go through. Press.
4. Screw hooks into place on each side of the cupboard space. Screw rings at each end of wire. Thread the wire through the top of the curtain.
6. Hang the curtain in place and put a marker pin at the required length. Take the fabric off the wire, measure from the top of the fabric to the marker pin. Measure the same length at three more points along the fabric, placing marker pins to mark the correct length. Cut the fabric 2.5cm (1in) below the marks. Take pins out. Make a hem and press (see the techniques section on hemming page 23).

If you are using two curtains, repeat the method above for the second curtain using the other piece of fabric.

Cup Cake Apron

The cup cake fabric on this simple apron works perfectly. It is important to use cotton or another fabric that washes easily. Thick fabrics can make an apron uncomfortable to wear. This apron can also be made using oilcloth. The photograph shows straps made of self fabric (the same fabric as the apron). These can also be made using tape or ribbon.

Techniques used
Hemming (page 23)   Patch Pockets (page 25)

> **MATERIALS TO BUY**
> **Fabric:**
> 115cm (45in) wide: 125cm (50in) long
> 150cm (60in) wide: 100cm (40in) long

Template on page 83

CUT SIZES / FINISHED MEASUREMENTS

Apron

CUT SIZES
Main piece: 88cm long × 60cm wide (34^1/$_2$in × 23^1/$_2$in)
Top width: 27cm (10^3/$_4$in)
Side length: 64cm (25^3/$_4$in)

FINISHED MEASUREMENTS
Main piece: 83cm long × 55cm wide (32^3/$_4$in × 21^3/$_4$in)
Top width: 22cm (8^3/$_4$in)
Side length: 59cm (23^1/$_4$in)

Straps

CUT SIZES
Neck: 53cm long × 8cm wide (21in × 3in)
Side: (cut two) 80cm long × 8cm wide (31^1/$_2$in × 3in) for a tie at the back or 104cm × 8cm (41in × 3in) if you prefer the straps to cross at the back and tie at the front

FINISHED MEASUREMENTS
Neck: 50cm long × 5cm wide (19^3/$_4$in × 2in)
Side: (each) 77cm long × 5cm wide (30^1/$_4$in × 2in) for a tie at the back or 101cm × 5cm (39^3/$_4$in × 2in) if you prefer the straps to cross at the back and tie at the front

Pocket

CUT SIZES
24cm deep × 33cm wide (9^1/$_2$in × 13in) sewn on 34cm (13^1/$_2$in) down from the top

FINISHED MEASUREMENTS
19cm deep × 28cm wide (7^1/$_2$in × 11in)

METHOD
1. Pin the pattern pieces to the fabric and cut them out.
2. Turn down the edges of the main part of the apron twice, making a very thin seam of approximately 1cm (^{3}/$_8$in) with no raw edge showing (pic 1) (see the techniques section on hemming page 23). Pin and sew with a straight stitch.

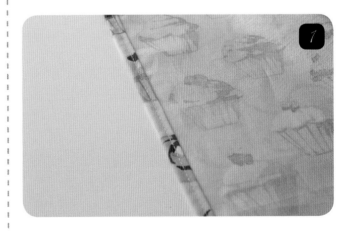

3. Turn down the top edge of the pocket twice in the same way, and sew using a straight stitch. Turn under the other three sides of the pocket once and press. Fold the pocket in half vertically and place a pin marker on the central line at the top and bottom.

4. Open out the pocket and place onto the apron, matching to the mark on the template. This should be placed 34cm (13$\frac{1}{2}$in) down from the top of the apron. Pin and sew using a straight stitch. Sew a small triangle in each top corner to strengthen (pic 2). Sew down the centre of the pocket (using the marker pins as a guide) with a straight stitch so you now have two pockets.

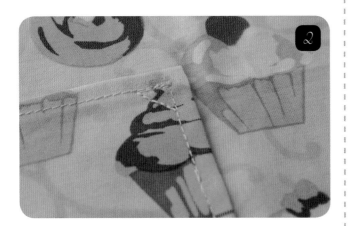

5. Cut three pieces of fabric for the ties and strap using the method in the techniques section on making ties on page 28 (pic 3). Sew ties and one side of neck strap in position as shown on the template on page 83.

6. Try the apron on and pin the second side of neck strap to size. When sewing place the neck strap and ties so that they are sewn onto a single layer of the main fabric, not on the top hem, so that the machine doesn't have to sew through too many layers of fabric.

This Suntop is made from a very light, pretty cotton print fabric and the Sundress is made from slightly thicker cotton. The lighter fabric works best for the top as it hangs better. The same pattern is used for the dress but with a longer piece of the same fabric for the bottom. Both are light, fresh and cool – great to wear on a hot summer's day.

Techniques used

Hemming (page 23)   Bias Binding (page 24)
Putting in Elastic (page 28)   Making Ties (page 28)

MATERIALS TO BUY

For the Suntop:
115cm (45in) wide: 150cm (60in) long
150cm (60in) wide: 125cm (50in) long
For the Sundress:
115cm (45in) wide: 180cm (71in) long
150cm (60in) wide: 180cm (71in) long

For the Sundress and Suntop:
2 hooks and eyes
Knicker or lightweight elastic: 60cm (23½in)
Bias Binding: 2cm wide x 150cm long (all sizes)
(³/₄in x 60in)

CUT SIZES	FINISHED MEASUREMENTS

Suntop and Sundress all sizes

Shoulder straps: (cut two) 8cm wide x 45cm long (3in x 17½in)	**Shoulder straps:** 2cm (³/₄in) wide, cut length to fit
Elastic: 50cm (19¾in) for front	

Suntop small

Top piece (front yoke): 45cm wide at top x 16.5cm deep at centre fold (17½in x 6½in)	**Top piece (front yoke):** 42cm wide at top x 13.5cm deep at centre fold (16½in x 5¼in)
Top piece (back yoke): 43.5cm wide at top x 13cm deep (17in x 5in)	**Top piece (back yoke):** 41cm wide at top x 10cm deep (16in x 4in)
Bottom pieces: (cut two – front & back alike) 65cm wide x 47cm long (25½in x 18¼in)	**Bottom pieces:** (front & back alike) 62cm (24¼in) wide, hem to required length

Suntop medium

Top piece (front yoke): 47cm wide at top x 17cm deep at centre fold (18¼in x 6¾in)	**Top piece (front yoke):** 44cm wide at top x 14cm deep at centre fold (17¼in x 5½in)
Top piece (back yoke): 47cm wide at top x 13cm deep (18¼in x 5in)	**Top piece (back yoke):** 44cm wide at top x 10cm deep (17¼in x 4in)
Bottom pieces: (cut two – front & back alike) 68cm wide x 47cm long (26¾in x 18½in)	**Bottom pieces:** (front & back alike) 65cm (25½in) wide, hem to required length

Suntop large

Top piece (front yoke): 49cm wide at top x 18.5cm deep at centre fold (19¼in x 7¼in)	**Top piece (front yoke):** 46cm wide at top x 15cm deep at centre fold (18in x 6in)
Top piece (back yoke): 49cm wide at top x 13.5cm deep (19¼in x 5¼in)	**Top piece (back yoke):** 46cm wide at top x 10.5cm deep (18in x 4¼in)
Bottom pieces: (cut two – front & back alike) 72cm wide x 47cm long (28¼in x 18¼in)	**Bottom pieces:** (front & back alike) 69cm (27in) wide, hem to required length

CUT SIZES	FINISHED MEASUREMENTS

Sundress small

Top piece (front yoke): 45cm wide at top x 16.5cm deep at centre fold (17½in x 6½in)	**Top piece (front yoke):** 42cm wide at top x 13.5cm deep at centre fold (16in x 5¼in)
Top piece (back yoke): 43.5cm wide at top x 13cm deep (17in x 5in)	**Top piece (back yoke):** 41cm wide at top x 10cm deep (16in x 4in)
Bottom pieces: (cut two – front & back alike) 65cm wide x 64cm long (25¾in x 25½in)	**Bottom pieces:** (front & back alike) 62cm (24¼in) wide, hem to required length

Sundress medium

Top piece (front yoke): 47cm wide at top x 17cm deep at centre fold (18½in x 6¾in)	**Top piece (front yoke):** 44cm wide at top x 14cm deep at centre fold (17¼in x 5½in)
Top piece (back yoke): 47cm wide at top x 13cm deep (18½in x 5in)	**Top piece (back yoke):** 44cm wide at top x 10cm deep (17¼in x 4in)
Bottom pieces: (cut two – front & back alike) 68cm wide x 64cm long (26¾in x 25½in)	**Bottom pieces:** (front & back alike) 65cm (25½in) wide, hem to required length

Sundress large

Top piece (front yoke): 49cm wide at top x 18.5cm deep at centre fold (19in x 7¼in)	**Top piece (front yoke):** 46cm wide at top x 15cm deep at centre fold (18in x 6in)
Top piece (back yoke): 49cm wide at top x 13.5cm deep (19¼in x 5¼in)	**Top piece (back yoke):** 46cm wide at top x 10.5cm deep (18in x 4¼in)
Bottom pieces: (cut two – front & back alike) 72cm wide x 64cm long (28³/₈in x 25½in)	**Bottom pieces:** (front & back alike) 69cm (27in) wide, hem to required length

Templates on page 83

METHOD

1. Place all the pattern pieces on the fabric, find your size and mark. Cut out the pieces.
2. Gather the front and back bottom pieces so that they are of equal widths in the following way. For the bottom piece, sew a line of stitches using the largest straight stitch possible on your machine along the longest (top) edge starting 4cm (1½in) in from each end and as near to the top raw edge as possible (pic 1). Tie off one end of the sewing line so that it's secure and leave the other end untied, so that you'll be able to gather the stitches. Put a marker pin halfway along the stitch line.

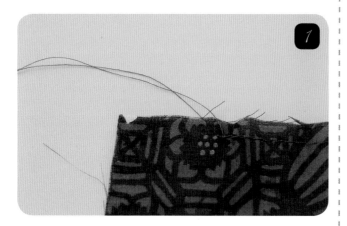

3. Put a marker pin in the centre of the top piece along the bottom edge. Take the yoke and place it on top of bottom piece, right sides together. Pin together in the centre at the top of both pieces by holding the two fabric pieces together at the marker pin points. Remove marker pins, repositioning one of the pins in the same place to hold both pieces of fabric together (pic 2). Also pin the pieces together at each end of the sewing line.

4. Take one end of the thread, pull and gather equally along the length, to fit the yoke. Pin the fabric evenly together along the edge.
5. Sew the gathered bottom piece onto the yoke using a straight stitch on the gathered side and using a 1.5cm (⅝in) seam from the top edge. Resize the stitching on your machine to the standard size for straight stitching. As you are stitching the gathers, stop every couple of centimetres (inches) and straighten up your top piece of fabric to stop the gathers from bunching. There will now be two stitch lines: one for the gathers and one for the seam.
6. Take out pins. Turn over and check your stitching for any mistakes.
7. Repeat stages 3–6 for the back bodice.
8. Now add the elastic by working on the yoke seam. Place a marker pin at the middle point of the elastic and another on the middle point of the seam. Pin the marker points together in the middle. Pin each end of the elastic to each end of the seam. Place in your machine and sew holding stitches at one end to keep the elastic in place.
9. Working on the first section of the fabric to the middle marker pin, stretch out the elastic to the same length as the fabric and sew using a zigzag stitch (pic 3). Then stretch the elastic again to the same length as the fabric and to the second marker pin and sew in place. Finish the raw edge of the fabric with pinking shears. (see the techniques section on elastic page 28).

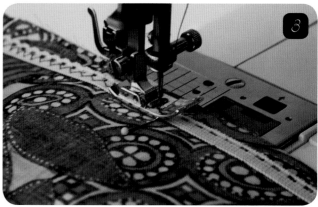

10. Pin the front and back side seams (right sides together). On the side without fastenings (right-hand side), sew down the complete seam.
11. On the side with fastenings, starting at the yoke seam, pin and sew the bottom side pieces together (leaving the yoke seam open).

12. Sew the bias binding on to the right side of both edges (see the techniques section on bias binding page 24), but without folding it on to the wrong side of the fabric. Cut another piece of bias binding the same length as the first piece. Pin on top of the wrong side of the fabric (pic 4). Sew along both top and bottom edges of the bias binding so that the bias binding sandwiches the fabric in place. This gives a neat edge and a place to where you can sew the hooks and eyes (pic 5). Sew across the base of the bias binding to secure it in place (pic 6).

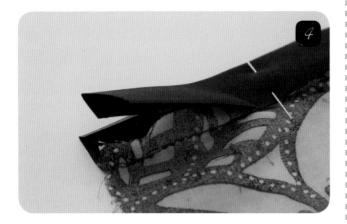

13. Finish all seams with pinking shears (see the techniques section on finishing edges and seams page 23).

14. For the straps see the techniques section on making ties page 28.

15. Pin the straps in position at the front only, on right side of fabric. Position each strap so that it hangs downwards making sure that one end of the strap is flush with the top edge of the yoke (pic 7).

16. With the right side facing and starting at the back, pin and sew the bias binding to the top of the dress, making sure that the straps at the front come between the binding and the yoke (pic 8). Take out the pins. Fold the bias binding over, so that it will be hidden from view when the dress is finished, and sew in place.

17. Try on the garment and pin the back of the straps to fit, bringing them towards the centre by approximately 2.5cm (1in) more than in the front, to prevent them from slipping off your shoulders. Pin and sew them in place over the top of the bias binding.

18. Hem the bottom of the garment to the required length (see the techniques section on hemming page 23).

19. Sew the hooks and eyes in place.

Embroidered Tablecloth and Napkins

This is a really easy pattern to make and yet creates something practical for your own home or a lovely present. You can personalise the tablecloth with embroidery. Use swirls, initials, flowers or a Christmas design for whatever the occasion.

Techniques used

Hemming (page 23)   Simple Embroidery (page 28)

MATERIALS TO BUY
For the tablecloth:
Measure your table and buy enough fabric to cover it, adding an extra 25cm (10in) for the drop on each side and another 2cm (³/₄in) for each hem.

For the napkins:
115cm (45in) wide: 70cm (28in) long – makes six
150cm (60in) wide: 35cm (14in) long – makes four

CUT SIZES

Napkins

Approximately 32cm (12¹/₂in) square

 Embroidery template on page 86

METHOD
1. Cut the fabric to size.
2. Turn over edges twice and hem with a straight stitch.
3. Mark the swirls for embroidery using tailor's chalk on the tablecloth and napkins, following the template on page 86.
4. Embroider your chosen motifs using embroidery thread and a running stitch (see the techniques section on simple embroidery page 28) (pic 1).
5. Wash everything in a washing machine according to the fabric washing instructions to remove the tailor's chalk.

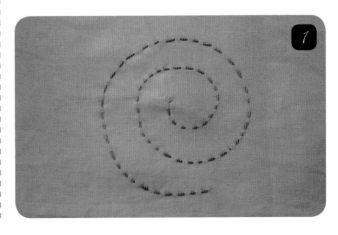

This dress is a comfortable and versatile garment that can be worn either on its own or over jeans or skirt. It works particularly well with a light cotton fabric and with a pretty floral print makes a perfect addition to your summer wardrobe. Don't be put off by the sleeves as the method is simple and uncomplicated.

Techniques used

Hemming (page 23)   Bias Binding (page 24)
Lace or Trimming (page 49)

MATERIALS TO BUY
Fabric:
115cm (45in) wide: 200cm (79in) long
150cm (60in) wide: 125cm (50in) long
Trimming: 150cm (60in) long
Bias binding: 2cm wide x 100cm long (^{5}/8in x 39in)
all sizes

CUT SIZES	FINISHED MEASUREMENTS
Small	
Back: 88cm long x 67cm wide at hem (34^3/4 x 26^1/4in)	**Back:** 87cm long x 65.5cm wide at hem (34in x 26in)
Front: 88.5cm long x 33.6cm wide at hem (34^3/4 x 13^1/4in)	**Front:** 87cm long x 32cm wide at hem (34in x 12½in)
Sleeves: 52cm wide at widest point x 20cm long (20^1/2in x 8in)	**Sleeves:** 17cm long x 16.5cm hem depth (6^3/4in x 6½in)
Medium	
Back: 89cm long x 69cm wide at hem (35in x 27in)	**Back:** 88cm long x 67.5cm wide at hem (34½in x 26½in)
Front: 89cm long x 34.5cm wide at hem (34^3/4 x 13½in)	**Front:** 88cm long x 33cm wide at hem (34½ in x 13in)
Sleeves: 52cm wide at widest point x 22cm long (20½in x 8^3/4in)	**Sleeves:** 19cm long x 14cm hem depth (7½in x 5½in)
Large	
Back: 90.5cm long x 72cm wide at hem (20^1/2in x 28^1/4in)	**Back:** 89cm long x 70.5cm wide at hem (35in x 28in)
Front: 90.5cm long x 36cm wide at hem (35^1/2in x 14in)	**Front:** 89cm long x 34.5cm wide at hem (35in x 13½in)
Sleeves: 52cm wide at widest point x 24cm long (20^1/2in x 9^1/2in)	**Sleeves:** 21cm long 15cm hem depth (8^1/4in x 6in)
All sizes	
Trimming: cut to length after main before sewing side seams	**Side ties:** (cut two) 1cm x 60cm (^{3}/8in x 23^1/2in)
Side ties: (cut two) 4cm x 63cm (1^1/2in x 24^3/4in)	

 Templates on page 86

METHOD

1. Pin the pieces of pattern to the fabric and cut out your size.
2. Pin and sew the front piece to the back piece at the shoulder seams, right sides together.
3. Press the seams open and finish the edges in your preferred style (see the techniques section on finishing edges and seams page 23).
4. For the sleeves, take one of your cut out sleeves and put a marker pin in the centre of the curved (top) edge. Match the marker pin to the shoulder seam (right sides together) and, working from the centre pin outwards, pin the sleeves to the sleeve edge of the dress
5. Sew in place and finish edges (pic 1).

6. Repeat for the other sleeve.
7. Try the dress on at this stage and measure the hem of the sleeves to the required length. Pin, press and sew the hems of both sleeves (see the techniques section on hemming page 23).
8. For the neck, with right side facing, start pinning the bias binding at the front V (see the techniques section on bias binding page 24). Allow 3cm (1¼in) overlap (pic 2). Continue pinning bias binding until you reach the shoulder seam. Pin the seam open and make a small fold of the bias binding at the seam (pic 3). Continue pinning bias binding until next seam, make another fold as before and continue pinning round to join the front V, finishing the bias binding without pinning the overlapping ends (pic 4).

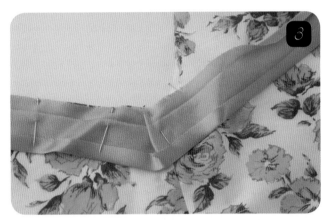

9. Starting at one side of the front V, sew along the folded edge of the bias binding to the other side of the V. If you turn your fabric and look at it on the other side, you should have a perfect V-shape sewing line. If the V is not perfect and your stitches are short of each other, make the V by taking one of the ends of thread and hand sew to meet the other stitches (pic 5).

10. To enable the binding to fold over neatly without bulking, cut the dress fabric down from the centre of the V to just above the stitch line (pic 6).

11. Fold over the bias binding, so it doesn't show on the right side, pin and stitch in place making sure you stitch the folds neatly and ensuring that the V is neat and overlapping. (pic 7). Take out all pins.

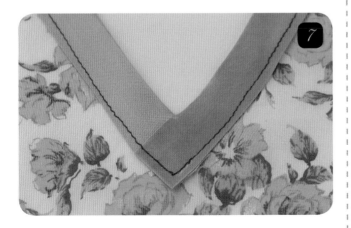

12. For the neck edging, pin the neck trim on the inside edge of the neck onto the bias binding. Cut to the correct length then pin and sew in place (pic 8).

13. Try on the dress again. At the front of the dress only, put a marker pin at the centre of the bottom bra line and another pin marker each side at the waist level. Take the dress off.

14. Place the fabric on a flat surface. Making sure the trim is placed equally on each side of the dress, pin and sew the trim onto the front of the dress from the side markers to the centre (pic 9).

15. Make the ties (see the techniques section on making ties page 23).
16. Pin the ties in place on the seam, placing one edge of the tie just above the edge of the trim.
17. Pin and sew the side seams, incorporating the ties.
18. Hem to the required length.

Using pretty fabric for the inside and the outside of this handy shopping bag gives you the option of turning it inside out to suit your colour scheme of the day.

If you are a compulsive shopper and are likely to buy lots of things you can reinforce the tops of the handles by stitching over the join of the straps to the bag twice.

Techniques used

Hemming (page 23)   Making Ties (page 28)

MATERIALS TO BUY
Main fabric and lining:
115cm (45in) wide: 50cm (20in) long of each
150cm (60in) wide: 50cm (20in) long of each

CUT SIZES	FINISHED MEASUREMENTS
Main fabric and lining	
(cut two of each) 36cm wide × 39.5cm long (14in × 15¹/₂in)	30cm wide × 33cm long (11³/₄in × 13in)
Straps	
(cut two of each) 61cm long × 6cm wide (24in × 2¹/₂in)	58cm long × 6cm wide (22³/₄in × 2¹/₂in)

 Template on page 84

METHOD

1. Mark the size of the main fabric and lining onto the fabric pieces and cut them out.
2. Main fabric: Pin the back and front pieces together, right sides facing, and sew with a straight stitch down the two sides and bottom with a 1.5cm (⁵/₈in) seam. Take out pins.
3. Repeat with the lining fabric.
4. Cut seams diagonally across the bottom corners of both the lining and the main fabric, being very careful not to cut into your stitches (see the techniques section on corners page 24).

5. Press all seams open on both the main fabric and the lining by pressing the seam down one side first (pic 1), then turning the fabric over and pressing open the other side of the seam (pic 2).

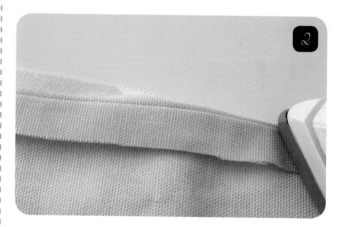

6. Turn the main fabric right side out, making sure the corners are neat and square.
7. Put your hand inside the lining fabric and slip the main fabric bag over the top of the lining, smoothing the creases and easing the two layers together. It is essential to spend some time getting the fabrics smooth and easing the two layers into the correct position.
8. Measure 33cm (13in) from the bottom of the bag and place a marker pin on each side and in the middle at the same points. Turn the bag over and repeat on the other side so there are now three pins on each side of the bag at the same point.
9. Turn under main fabric at marker points and take out the marker pins. Pin in place.

10. Fold lining fabric to meet fold on main fabric, making sure that lining and main fabric are exactly the same height (pic 3). Press.

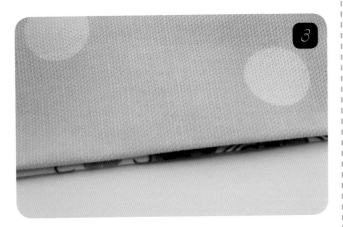

11. For the straps, fold the lining fabric lengthways a quarter of the width. Press. Fold the other side to match (pic 4). Press again.

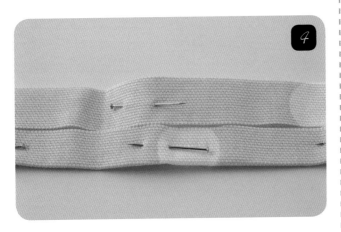

12. Repeat using the main fabric.
13. Put both straps together with folded edges and all raw edges on the inside. Pin together in place. Sew down each edge of strap as near to the edge as possible (pic 5).

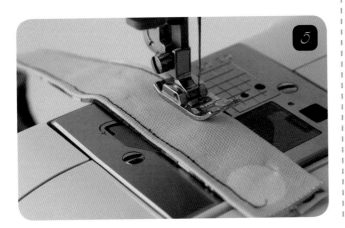

14. Match the main fabric of the strap to the main fabric of the bag and sandwich the end of the strap between the lining and main fabric by placing it 8cm (3in) in from the edge of the bag and approx 2.5cm (1in) down between the two layers (pic 6).

15. Turn the bag over, pin and insert second strap 8cm (3in) in from the same edge as the first strap (on the opposite side). Measure straps and check they are of equal length. Reposition them if necessary. Sandwich strap end between lining and main fabric as before. Pin loose end of first strap at other end of bag 8cm (3in) in from the other edge, making sure main fabric is facing outwards and strap is not twisted. Insert as before 2.5cm (1in) down and pin. Repeat with second strap.
16. Sew all around the top edge, as near to the top edge as possible, enclosing the straps as you go (pic 7). Press.

Comfy Slouch Trousers – for women and men

These slouch trousers couldn't be easier to make. Use any cosy fabric of your choice. They're perfect for slouching around the house, and so comfortable that you won't want to take them off. Use any type of fabric: light cotton for summer and thicker fabric for winter in either florals, stripes, tartans or polka dots.

Techniques used

Clipping Seams (page 24) Waistband Casing (page 24)

 Templates on pages 90 and 91

> **MATERIALS TO BUY**
> *For the women's trousers:*
> 115cm (45in) wide: 230cm (90in) long
> 150cm (60in) wide: 230cm (90in) long
>
> *For the men's trousers:*
> 115cm (45in) wide: 250cm (100in) long
> 150cm (60in) wide: 250cm (100in) long

FOR WOMEN

CUT SIZES	FINISHED MEASUREMENTS
Small	
(cut two of each piece) **Back:** 111cm long × 39.5cm at widest point (43³/₄in × 15¹/₂in) **Front:** 111cm long × 32cm at widest point (43³/₄in × 12¹/₂in)	Hem to length required **Back:** 36.5cm (14¹/₄in) at widest point **Front:** 29cm (11¹/₂in) at widest point
Medium	
(cut two of each piece) **Back:** 111cm long × 41cm at widest point (43³/₄in × 16in) **Front:** 111cm long × 34cm at widest point (43³/₄in × 13¹/₂in)	Hem to length required **Back:** 38cm (15in) at widest point **Front:** 31cm (12in) at widest point
Large	
(cut two of each piece) **Back:** 111cm long: 43cm at widest point (43³/₄in × 17in) **Front:** 111cm long × 36.5cm at widest point (43³/₄in × 14¹/₄in)	Hem to length required **Back:** 40cm (15³/₄in) at widest point **Front:** 33cm (13in) at widest point
Tie (all sizes)	
175cm length × 5cm wide (68³/₄in × 2in)	172cm long × 1.5cm wide (67³/₄in × ⁵/₈in)

FOR MEN

CUT SIZES	FINISHED MEASUREMENTS
Small	
(cut two of each piece) **Back:** 118cm long × 46cm at widest point (46¹/₂in × 18in) **Front:** 118cm long × 35cm at widest point (46¹/₂in × 13³/₄in)	Hem to length required **Back:** 43cm (17in) at widest point **Front:** 32cm (12¹/₂in) at widest point
Medium	
(cut two of each piece) **Back:** 118cm long × 49.5cm at widest point (46¹/₂in × 19¹/₂in) **Front:** 118cm long × 37.5cm at widest point (46¹/₂in × 14³/₄in)	Hem to length required **Back:** 46.5cm (18¹/₄in) at widest point **Front:** 36cm (14in) at widest point
Large	
(cut two of each piece) **Back:** 118cm long × 53.5cm at widest point (46¹/₂in × 21in) **Front:** 118cm long × 41cm at widest point (46¹/₂in × 16in)	Hem to length required **Back:** 50.5cm (20in) at widest point **Front:** 38cm (15in) at widest point
Tie (all sizes)	
175cm length × 5cm wide (68³/₄in × 2in)	172cm long × 1.5cm wide (67³/₄in × ⁵/₈in)

METHOD

To make either the women's or the men's trousers:

1. Select your size, pin the pattern pieces onto the fabric and cut out.

2. Pin both front pieces (right sides) together along the curved edge, (crotch) and sew a 1.5cm (5/8in) seam with a straight stitch. To reinforce this seam, sew another row of stitches on top of the first.

3. Repeat this for the back.

4. Clip the fabric at the curves up to the stitches, being careful not to cut through them (see the techniques section on clipping seams page 24).

5. Pin and sew front and back (right sides together) using a 1.5cm (5/8in) seam on both outside edges.

6. Starting at the crotch centre and working down each leg, pin and sew the inside leg seams, right sides together. Open all seams flat and press.

7. To make the waistband, measure and mark with marker pins 5cm (2in) down from the raw edge at the waist (pic 1).

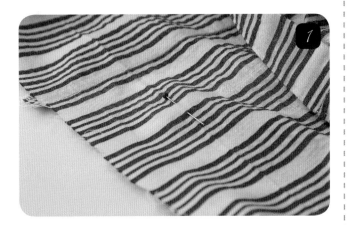

8. Fold down at marker pin points and press (pic 2). Open out the fold, remove the marker pins and fold the edge to the crease line.

9. Fold over from the crease line with the raw edges already tucked under, press again and pin (pic 3).

10. Sew as near to each edge of the waistband as possible (pic 4).

11. Very carefully with a seam ripper open a seam between the two casing stitch lines, either at the centre or at one side depending on where you want your drawstring (pic 5).

12. Using the cut fabric for the waistband tie (see the techniques section on making ties page 28), fold the fabric in half lengthways, press, open out flat and fold both raw edges to the centre line, fold in half again, (you should now have four thicknesses) press and sew along the open edge (pic 6).

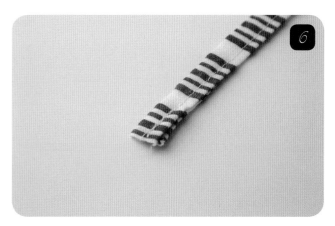

13. Thread the drawstring through the waistband and even up the ties equally.
14. Sew a holding line of stitches on the waistband opposite the drawstring exit point (pic 7). This stops the ties from slipping out.

15. Pin hem to fit and sew with a straight stitch (see the techniques section on hemming page 23).

A fashionable belt or scarf can be made with any type of fabric. This is an excellent and easy first project and demonstrates how a beautiful piece of fabric can easily transform your look.

Techniques used
Hemming (page 23)

> **MATERIALS TO BUY**
> **Fabric:**
> 115cm (45in) wide: 30cm (10in) long
> 150cm (60in) wide: 30cm (10in) long

CUT SIZES

Cut two pieces: 13cm wide × 110cm long (5in × 43in)

FINISHED MEASUREMENTS

10cm wide × 205cm long (4in × 80½in)

Template on page 84

METHOD

1. Pin the pattern onto the fabric and cut two equal pieces. Join the two pieces of fabric together in the middle by pinning and sew with a 1.5cm (⅝in) seam. Finish edges by your chosen method (see techniques section on finishing edges and seams page 23). Open the seam and press (pic 1).

2. Pin the hem all the way round by turning the fabric over twice (pic 2). Make the smallest hem possible (see the techniques section on hemming page 23).

3. Sew with a straight stitch.

Flirty Flared Skirt

This modern, light skirt is made in a pretty broderie anglais fabric. It's easy to make and comfortable to wear. It has ties to secure and fasten it and makes a perfect summer skirt.

Techniques used

Hemming (page 23) Bias Binding (page 24)
Making Ties (page 28)

MATERIALS TO BUY
Fabric:
115cm (45in) wide: 180cm (71in) long
150cm (60in) wide: 120cm (48in) long

Bias Binding: 2cm wide x 125cm long (³/₄in x 50in) all sizes

Notes on cut sizes

A = underwrap yoke (shorter width)
B = back and front yoke (longer width)
C = underwrap skirt (one side flared, one side straight)
D = back and front flared skirt (curved both sides)

Cut one piece of A
Cut two pieces of B
Cut one piece of C
Cut two pieces of D on fold

Cut A, B and C on the grain of fabric
Place the fold of D on the grain of fabric and, as you're cutting out, this will cut across the grain, which gives the fabric some stretch when assembling the skirt.

As the pieces are curved, measurements are taken at the top straight edge across each piece.

Templates on page 87

CUT SIZES

Small

Underwrap yoke (A): 28.5cm wide x 18cm deep (11¹/₄in x 7in)
Back and front yoke (B): 40cm wide x 18cm deep (15³/₄in x 7in)
Underwrap skirt (C): 37cm wide x 25cm deep (14¹/₂in x 10in)
Back and front flared skirt (D): 21.5cm wide x 25cm deep (8¹/₂in x 10in)

Medium

Underwrap yoke (A): 34cm wide x 18cm deep (13¹/₂in x 7in)
Back and front yoke (B): 44cm wide x 18cm deep (17¹/₄in x 7in)
Underwrap skirt (C): 40.5cm wide x 25cm deep (16in x 10in)
Back and front flared skirt (D): 23cm wide x 25cm deep (9in x 10in)

Large

Underwrap yoke (A): 38cm wide x 18cm deep (15in x 7in)
Back and front yoke (B): 47.5cm wide x 18cm deep (18³/₄in x 7in)
Underwrap skirt (C): 45cm wide x 25cm deep (17¹/₂in x 10in)
Back and front flared skirt (D): 25cm wide x 25cm deep (10in x 10in)

Ties

cut four pieces 4cm x 40cm (1¹/₂in x 15³/₄in)

FINISHED MEASUREMENTS

Small

Underwrap yoke (A): 25cm wide x 15cm deep (10in x 6in)
Back and front yoke (B): 37cm wide x 15cm deep (14¹/₂ in x 6in)
Underwrap skirt (C): 34cm (13¹/₂in) wide, hem to required length
Back and front flared skirt (D): 18.5cm (7¹/₄in) wide, hem to required length

Medium

Underwrap yoke (A): 31.5cm wide x 15cm deep (12¹/₄in x 6in)
Back and front yoke (B): 41cm wide x 15cm deep (16in x 6in)
Underwrap skirt (C): 37.5cm (14³/₄in) wide, hem to required length
Back and front flared skirt (D): 20cm (8in) wide, hem to required length

Large

Underwrap yoke (A): 35cm wide x 15cm deep (13³/₄in x 6in)
Back and front yoke (B): 44.5cm wide x 15cm deep (17¹/₂in x 6in)
Underwrap skirt (C): 42cm (16¹/₂in) wide, hem to required length
Back and front flared skirt (D): 22cm (8³/₄in) wide, hem to required length

Ties

1cm x 38cm (³/₈in x 15in)

METHOD

1. Select the size you want and place the pattern pieces on the fabric. Cut them out, taking note of where to cut on fold, also placing the pattern on the grain of the fabric.

2. Pin and sew piece A to piece C and pieces B to D right sides together (see diagram below) (see the techniques section on seams page 22).

3. Pin and sew all skirt pieces together as shown.

		inside tie		outside tie	
end	FRONT YOKE **B**	BACK YOKE **B**		UNDERWRAP YOKE **A**	end
	FRONT FLARED SKIRT **D**	BACK FLARED SKIRT **D**		UNDERWRAP SKIRT **C**	

Ties are sewn onto points shown

4. Hem two outside edges (see the techniques section on hemming page 23).

5. Pin and sew the bias binding to the waist of the skirt. At the ends, fold the bias binding in (pic 1). Leave both ends open so you can insert the ties (pic 2) (see the techniques section on bias binding page 24).

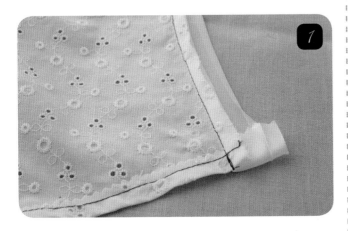

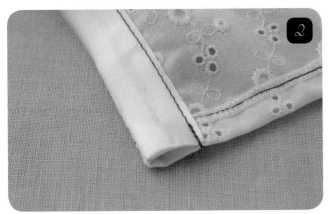

6. Pin and sew the ties to the positions shown in the diagram by easing the ties at least 1.3cm (¹/₂ in) into the gap between the bias binding and the fabric (sew over the top of the existing stitch line) (pic 3).

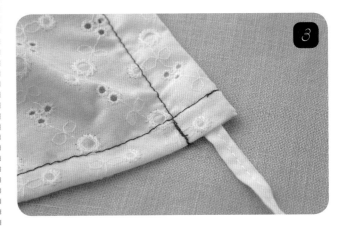

7. Hem to the required length, then finish the raw edges.

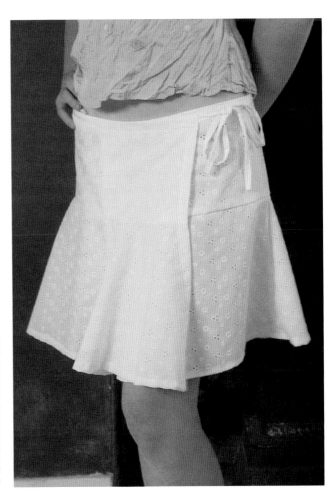

You can make this simple garment look really attractive by using a beautiful piece of fabric. You can also make a one-colour fabric come alive by adding sequins or beads.

Techniques used

Hemming (page 23)   Making Ties (page 28)
Beads and Sequins (page 29)

MATERIALS TO BUY

Fabric:
115cm (45in) wide: 150cm (60in) long
150cm (60in) wide: 125cm (50in) long

Beads and sequins to decorate

METHOD

1. Cut out the pieces for the sarong and the straps.
2. Turn over the edges of the sarong twice, and sew hems with a straight stitch (see the techniques section on hemming page 23).
3. Make the straps (see the techniques section on making ties page 28). Pin the straps to the top of the garment behind the main pieces on the wrong side. Then sew (pic 1).
4. Press all seams after sewing.
5. Hand sew sequins and beads to decorate the garment (see the techniques section on beads and sequins page 23).

CUT SIZES	FINISHED MEASUREMENTS
Sarong	
115cm (45in) wide: (cut 2 pieces) 78cm wide × 75cm long (30³/₄in × 30in) 150cm (60in) wide: use full width of fabric	115cm (45in) width: 73cm long × 150cm wide (28³/₄in × 60in) 150cm (60in) width: 147cm wide × 70cm long (58in × 27¹/₂in)
Straps	
(cut two) 103cm long × 13cm wide (40¹/₂in × 5in)	100cm long × 4cm wide (39¹/₄in × 1¹/₂in)

These shorts can be made in denim or in a medium-weight cotton or linen; they are comfortable, easy wearing and trendy. The method is the same as the slouch trousers on page 51 except for the turn-ups and pocket. These are made with a drawstring waist, but work just as well with elastic threaded through the casing.

Use any type of fabric: light cotton for summer and thicker fabric for winter in either florals, stripes, tartans or polka dots.

Techniques used

Hemming (page 23)   Waistband Casing (page 24)
Patch Pockets (page 25)

MATERIALS TO BUY
Fabric:
115cm (45in) wide: 160cm (63in) long
150cm (60in) wide: 160cm (63in) long

METHOD

1. Find your size, and place the pattern pieces onto the fabric. Pin the pattern pieces onto the fabric and cut out. Don't cut the turn-up fabric until you have finished sewing the legs of the shorts.

2. Pin both the front pieces (right sides) together along the curved edge (crotch) and sew with a straight stitch with a 1.5cm (5/8in) seam. To reinforce the crotch seam sew another row of stitches on top of the first. Repeat this for the back.

3. Clip fabric at curves up to the stitches taking care not to cut through them (see the techniques section on clipping seams page 24).

4. Pin and sew the front and back (right sides together) with a 1.5cm (5/8in) seam on both outside edges. Open all seams flat and press.

5. To make the waistband, measure and mark with marker pins 5cm (2in) down from the raw edge at the waist. Fold down at the marker pin points and press. Open out the fold, remove marker pins and fold the edge to the crease line. Fold over from the crease line with the raw edges already tucked under and press again (pic 1).

CUT SIZES | **FINISHED MEASUREMENTS**

Small

Front: (cut two) 73cm long × 35cm at widest point (28³/₄in × 13³/₄in)
Back: 73cm long × 46cm at widest point (28³/₄in × 18in)

Fronts: 32cm (12¹/₂in) at widest point
Back: 43cm (17in) at widest point

Medium

Front: (cut two) 73cm long × 37.5cm at widest point (28³/₄in × 14³/₄in)
Back: 73cm long × 49.5cm at widest point (28³/₄in × 19¹/₂in)

Fronts: 36cm (14in) at widest point
Back: 46.5cm (18¹/₄in) at widest point

Large

Front: (cut two) 73cm long × 41cm at widest point (28³/₄in × 16in)
Back: 73cm long × 53cm at widest point (28³/₄in × 21in)

Fronts: 38cm (15in) at widest point
Back: 50.5cm (20in) at widest point

Pocket (all sizes)

20cm deep × 16.5cm wide (8in × 6¹/₂in)

16cm deep × 13.5cm wide (6¹/₄in × 5¹/₄in) – positioned on side seam centrally placed on left leg, starts 29cm (11¹/₂in) down from top

Tie

175cm long × 5cm wide (68³/₄in × 2in)

172cm long × 1.5cm wide (67³/₄in × 5/8in)

Turn-ups

12cm (4³/₄in) deep × widest width of bottom of shorts (measure when main piece is finished)

4.5cm (1³/₄in) deep

 Templates on page 92

6. Stitch two sewing lines as close to each edge of the waistband as possible (pic 2).

7. Very carefully with a seam ripper open a seam between the two casing stitch lines, either at the centre or at one side depending on where you want your drawstring (pic 3).

8. Using your cut piece of fabric make a drawstring (tie), (see the techniques section on making ties page 28).
9. Sew a hold line of stitches on the waistband opposite the drawstring exit point (pic 4). This will stop the ties from slipping out.

10. For the pockets fold and press the two longest sides and the bottom.
11. Fold the top of the pocket over twice 1.3cm ($^1/_2$in). Press. Sew across the top (pic 5).

12. Fold the pocket in half lengthways and put a marker pin in the centre at the top and bottom.
13. Open out the pocket and place onto the shorts on the right side of the fabric on one of the legs by matching marker pins to the centre of the side seam. Pin in place and stitch the two sides and the bottom, leaving the top open (pic 6).

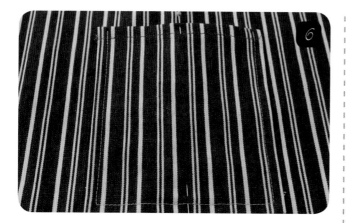

14. Pin and sew inside leg seams, starting at the centre of the crotch and working down each leg.

15. To make the turn-ups, measure the width of the bottom of the shorts and double it to allow for the front and back. Cut two pieces of fabric (one for each leg) adding 2.5cm (1in) each side to allow for the seams.

16. Take the exact measurement of the width of the bottom of the shorts. Lay the turn-up fabric on top of the bottom of the shorts and mark the turn-up accurately with a pin, allowing for a 1.5cm (⅝in) seam (pic 7). Pin and stitch the seam to make a circle of fabric (pic 8).

17. Open out the seam and fold the turn-up in half lengthways so that the right side is showing on both the inside and the outside of the turn-up (pic 9).

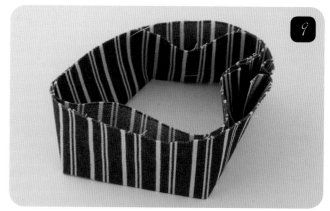

18. Pull the shorts inside out. Slip the turn-ups over the bottom of the shorts. Match the seam of the turn-up to the inside seam of the shorts. Pin and sew (pic 10). Repeat with the other leg.

19. Turn the shorts the right way out again. Bring the turn-ups out, turning up and over. Press (pic 11). Put a hand stitch on each side of the turn-up to hold in place.

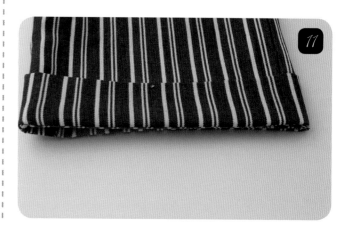

This is a very easy-to-follow method for making knickers or bikini bottoms. By choosing some beautiful fabric and ribbons these make fantastic gifts. Make sure you choose a lightweight fabric or you could feel as though you're wearing a nappy.

Techniques used

Top stitching elastic (page 28)   Lace or trimming (page 29)

MATERIALS TO BUY

Fabric:

115cm (45in) wide: 50cm (20in) long

150cm (60in) wide: 50cm (20in) long

Elastic (all sizes): 150cm (60in) long

Ribbon: 2m (79in) 1.5cm-wide (⅝in) ribbon for sides, 25cm (10in) 1cm-wide (⅜in) ribbon for front

Templates on page 82

CUT SIZES	FINISHED MEASUREMENTS
Small	
Back: 26cm long × 32cm wide at top (10¼in × 14in)	**Back:** 24cm long × 34cm wide at top (9½in × 13½in)
Front: 19cm long × 23.5cm wide at top (7½in × 9¼in)	**Front:** 17.5cm long × 22cm wide at top (7in × 8¾in)
Gusset: (cut two) 15.5cm long × 15.5cm wide at top × 8cm wide at bottom (6in × 6in × 3in)	**Gusset:** 14cm long × 14cm wide at top × 6.5cm wide at bottom (5½in × 5½in × 2½in)
Elastic*	
Leg edges: (cut two) 38cm (15in)	
Top back: 22cm (8¾in)	
Top front: 14cm (5½in)	
Medium	
Back: 27cm long × 34cm wide at top (10¾in × 13½in)	**Back:** 25cm long × 32.5cm wide at top (10in × 12¾in)
Front: 20cm long × 25cm wide at top (8in × 10in)	**Front:** 18.5cm long × 24cm wide at top (7¼in × 9½in)
Gusset: (cut two) 15.5cm long × 15.5cm wide at top × 8cm wide at bottom (6in × 6in × 3in)	**Gusset:** 14cm long × 14cm wide at top × 6.5cm wide at bottom (5½in × 5½in × 2½in)
Elastic*	
Leg edges: (cut two) 40cm (16in)	
top back: 24cm (11in)	
top front: 16cm (6in)	
Large	
Back: 28cm long × 36cm wide at top (11in × 12½in)	**Back:** 26.5cm long × 30.5cm wide at top (10½in × 12in)
Front: 21cm long × 27.5cm wide at top (8¼in × 10¾in)	**Front:** 19.5cm long × 26cm wide at top (7¾in × 10¼in)
Gusset: (cut two) 15.5cm long × 15.5cm wide at top × 8cm wide at bottom (6in × 6in × 3in)	**Gusset:** 14cm long × 14cm wide at top × 6.5cm wide at bottom (5½in × 5½in × 2½in)
Elastic*	
Leg edges: (cut two) 42cm (17in)	
top back: 26cm (12in)	
top front: 18cm (7in)	

* These are all relaxed lengths, they will stretch as you sew them on to fit the appropriate edges

Ribbon Ties (all sizes)

Cut four lengths of 1.5cm (⅝in) wide ribbon to 40cm (15¾in) each

Ribbon Trims

Cut one length of 1cm (⅜in) wide ribbon to 25cm (10in)

METHOD

1. Find your size and cut out the pieces on the fabric.

TIP

On some fabrics, and probably on the fabric you are using here, there is no right or wrong side, so mark the right side with a little coloured sticker.

2. Take both gusset pieces and place them so they are matching right sides together. Take the shortest edge of the back piece and the longest edge of the gusset, sandwich the large piece between the two small pieces and pin in place (pic 1).

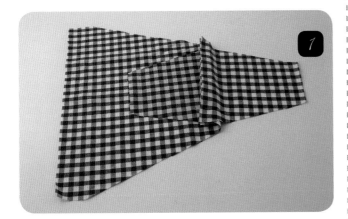

3. Sew a 1.5cm (⅝in) seam across the top of the pins (pic 2).

4. Remove pins. Open out one side of the gusset so that right sides of one gusset piece and the back piece are facing. Roll from the longest edge of the back piece of fabric up to the seam (pic 3).

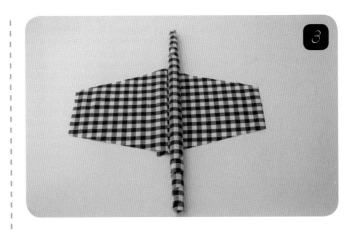

5. Place the shortest edge of front piece on top of one piece of gusset, right sides together (pic 4).

6. Take the other piece of gusset and pull it over to meet the other edges making a sandwich, then pin along the edge (pic 5).

7. Sew a 1.5cm (⅝in) seam across the pins.

8. Turn the gusset inside out (folding it towards you so that right sides are facing). All the raw edges should now be on the inside (pic 6).

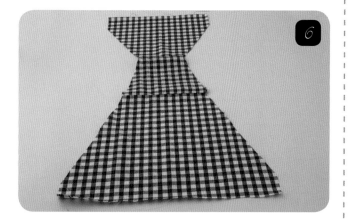

9. Fold all raw edge seams 1cm (³⁄₈in) and press.
10. Mark centre point on longest edge of back and front.
11. To attach the elastic pin one end of the elastic to the outside edge of the back, place in the machine (see the techniques section on top stitching elastic page 28). Change the setting to zigzag stitch and make a secure stitch at the beginning to hold the edge of the elastic in place.
12. With the machine needle down, holding the elastic in place, pin the other end of the elastic to other end of the back piece of fabric (pic 7).

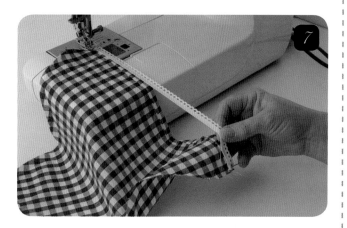

13. Find the centre of the elastic and the centre of the back piece of fabric and put a marker pin in each. Pin the elastic to the halfway marker point on the back piece of the knickers. Stretch the elastic in place and sew to the halfway point.
14. Stretch the elastic from the halfway point to the end and sew in place (pic 8).

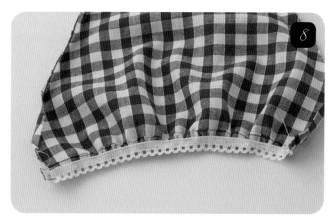

15. Repeat on the other three sides.
16. Cut four pieces of ribbon. Before attaching it, change the colour of your thread if necessary. Fold over one end of the ribbon 1.3cm (¹⁄₂in) and pin in place at each corner on either the right or wrong side at the back and at the front and sew in place (pic 9).

17. Using the narrower ribbon, make a bow and hand sew in place in the middle on the front of the knickers (pic 10).

Based on the idea of a patchwork, these stitched vintage handkerchiefs make a unique style of curtain. Vintage handkerchiefs are generally made from light, sheer fabrics and are perfect to decorate a small window as the light shines through the fabric highlighting the detail. Use organza ribbon as tie-ups for a pretty, delicate effect if required. Vintage handkerchiefs can be bought from second-hand, charity shops, eBay or found in your grandmother's cupboard. If you can't find any vintage handkerchiefs use the same method with scraps of fabric. Cut out squares of equal sizes and sew them together to create the size of fabric that fits your window. You can also hand sew the handkerchiefs together.

MATERIALS TO BUY
Measure your window or space and buy enough square handkerchiefs to cover it.
100cm (40in) organza ribbon (if ties are required, see method below)

METHOD

1. If possible, use handkerchiefs that are all the same size for these curtains. Press each handkerchief. If they are old or very fine press or steam them gently to get the creases out.

2. Lay the handkerchiefs out in horizontal lines on a flat surface in the order you want them. Make sure you have enough to cover the size of your window.

3. Pin the handkerchiefs together with right sides facing, place one handkerchief on top of the other so that it overlaps about 2mm ($^1/_{16}$in). This can be a bit fiddly so spend time and use plenty of pins to keep the fabric straight. Keep the lacy or detailed edges on the right side. Pin them in horizontal sections first, ensuring that each line of handkerchiefs is exactly the same width.

4. Set your machine to either zigzag or straight stitch and sew the handkerchiefs together with right sides always facing to show off any pretty edgings.

5. If you want curtain ties, cut two or three ribbon lengths to double the drop size of the curtain. If you don't want ties then hang the curtain as in 11 and 12.

6. If you are using ribbon to tie up the curtain fold the ribbon in half end to end and at the crease place over the top of the curtain.

7. Pin in place at the top with one end draping at the back and one end draping at the front.

8. Stitch across the ribbon and back again. Take out pins.

9. Repeat with the other lengths of ribbon in equal spacing across the curtain.

10. Fold the bottom end of the ribbon in half and cut upwards from the outside corners of the ribbon to make a 'V'.

11. Attach curtain pincer clips to the curtain and hang from the curtain pole.

12. Either pull back the curtain in place with rings or pull up the fabric and tie with ribbon bows when required.

This bag is made from deckchair fabric (which is 45cm (17¾in) wide) so it's durable and hardwearing. It's big enough to carry a towel, bikini and any other vital things needed for the beach. We've made this bag with punched eyelets for the handles, but if you can't get hold of an eyelet machine, simply attach the handles on the inside of the bag by stitching to the top edge of the bag.

Techniques used

Hemming (page 23)   Corners (page 24)
Making ties (page 28)

MATERIALS TO BUY
Fabric:
Deckchair 45cm (17¾in) wide: 110cm (44in) long
Or other 115cm (45in) wide: 75cm (30in) long
150cm (60in) wide: 75cm (30in) long
Eyelets: 4 x 4cm (1½in)

Template on page 85

CUT SIZES	FINISHED MEASUREMENTS
Fabric	
(cut two) 51.5cm wide x 46cm long (20¼in x 18in)	47cm wide x 38cm long (18¼in x 15in)
Handles	
(cut two) 69cm long x 6cm wide (27in x 2½in)	65cm long x 3cm wide (25in x 1¼in)

METHOD
1. Pin the pattern pieces onto the fabric and cut them out.
2. Place right sides together. Pin and sew up sides and bottom.
3. Open out all seams and press.
4. Put your hand into a bottom corner of the bag, open out the corner by spreading your hand (pic 1). Feel down with other hand to match up the seams. When one seam is on top of the other, place a pin across the corner to hold in it place.
5. Repeat on the other side.

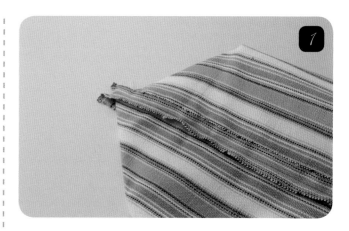

6. Place on a flat surface and measure 8cm (3in) down the seam line from the corner, then place a pin marker (pic 2).

7. At the pin marker, using a ruler, mark your sewing line with tailor's chalk 15cm (6in) across (pic 3). Pin and sew along the tailor's chalk line.

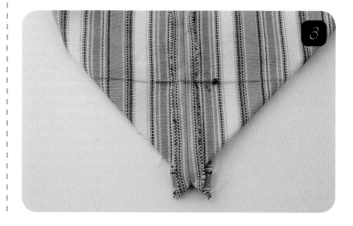

8. Repeat on the other side.

9. Trim the corners with pinking shears (pic 4).
10. For the top hem, turn over the top edge and make a 1.5cm ($^{5}/_{8}$in) hem.
11. Working on the wrong side, fold down the top 10cm (4in) (pic 5). Pin and press, then sew a top stitch line as close to the folded edge as possible (pic 6).

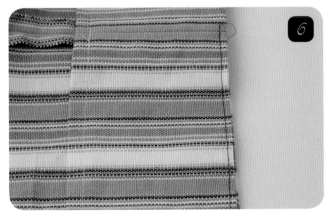

12. Turn right side out and put in the eyelets as marked on the template (page 85).

13. Make two ties (see the techniques section on making ties page 28).
14. Put the handles through the eyelets and stitch in place. The wrong side of the strap should be facing the wrong side of the bag (pic 7).

Dazzling Wraparound Top

This versatile top looks fantastic over jeans. Use a light cotton to make it hang nicely and use either fabric or ribbon for the ties. In the photograph we have used dark thread for the stitching so that it's easy to see. When sewing your garment use thread that matches your fabric.

Techniques used

Hemming (page 23)   Bias binding (page 24)

Gathering (page 25)   Adding ties (page 28)

MATERIALS TO BUY

Fabric:

115cm (45in) wide: 225cm (89in) long

150cm (60in) wide: 150cm (60in) long

Bias binding: 2cm wide x 200cm long (³/₄in x 79in) all sizes

METHOD

1. Select your size. Pin pattern pieces on the fabric and cut them out. For the top front piece, cut one side out first and then flip over the template and cut out the second piece, this creates a mirror image of the first piece.

2. Take the bottom section of the front piece and sew a gather line, setting your machine to use the longest stitch possible (see the techniques section on gathering page 25). To avoid too much gathering under the arms and at the bust, start the gather line 5cm (2in) in from each end (pic 1). Gather the fabric so that it matches the same length as the bottom edge of the top piece.

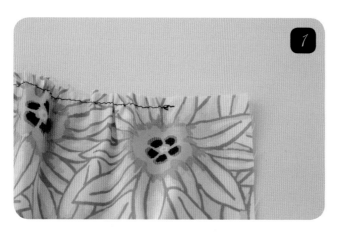

CUT SIZES	FINISHED MEASUREMENTS
Small	
Bottom front: (cut two) 38cm wide x 53cm long (15in x 21in)	**Bottom front:** 35cm wide x 50cm long (13¾in x 19¾in)
Bottom back: 64cm wide x 53cm long (25¾in x 21in)	**Bottom back:** 61cm wide x 50cm long (24in x 19¾in)
Top front: 28.5cm long x 30.5cm widest point at bottom (11¼in x 12in)	**Top front:** 27cm long x 29.5cm widest point at bottom (10¾in x 11½in)
Top back: 26cm long x 51cm widest point at bottom (10¼in x 20in)	**Top back:** 24.5cm long x 49.5cm widest point at bottom (9½in x 19½in)
Sleeves: 19cm long at centre fold x 49cm at widest point (8in x 19¼in)	**Sleeves:** 17cm long at centre x 14cm width at widest point when laid flat (6½in x 5½in)
Medium	
Bottom front: (cut two) 42cm wide x 54cm long (16½in x 21¼in)	**Bottom front:** 39cm wide x 51cm long (15¼in x 20in)
Bottom back: 68cm wide x 54cm long (26¾in x 21¼in)	**Bottom back:** 65cm wide x 51cm long (25½in x 20in)
Top front: 28.5cm long x 32.5cm widest point at bottom (11¼in x 12¾in)	**Top front:** 27.5cm long x 32cm widest point at bottom (10¾in x 12½in)
Top back: 26cm long x 53cm widest point at bottom (10¼in x 21in)	**Top back:** 24cm long x 51.5cm widest point at bottom (9½in x 20¼in)
Sleeves: 20cm long at centre fold x 49cm at widest point (8in x 19¼in)	**Sleeves:** 18cm long at centre x 14cm width at widest point when laid flat (7in x 5½in)
Large	
Bottom front: (cut two) 45cm wide x 55cm long (17½in x 21¾in)	**Bottom front:** 42cm wide x 52cm long (16½in x 20½in)
Bottom back: 71cm wide x 55cm long (28in x 21¾in)	**Bottom back:** 68cm wide x 52cm long (28¾in x 20½in)
Top front: 28.5cm long x 34cm widest point at bottom (11¼in x 13½in)	**Top front:** 27cm long x 30.5cm widest point at bottom (10¾in x 12in)
Top back: 25cm long x 56cm widest point at bottom (10in x 22in)	**Top back:** 24cm long x 54.5cm widest point at bottom (9½in x 21½in)
Sleeves: 21cm long at centre fold x 49cm at widest point (8¼in x 19¼in)	**Sleeves:** 18cm long at centre x 14.5cm width at widest point when laid flat (7in x 5¾in)
All sizes	
Ties: (make four) 4cm x 65cm (1½in x 25½in)	**Ties:** (make four) 1cm x 63cm (³/₈in x 24½in)

 Templates on page 88

Once you have gathered, pin and sew the front top to the front bottom piece, right sides together (pic 2). Repeat this process for the other front section.

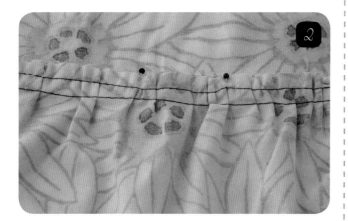

3. Repeat for the back, pin and sew the top to the bottom piece, gathering as before. Finish off the raw edges as you choose (see the techniques section on finishing edges and seams page 23).
4. Pin and sew the shoulder seams, then finish the raw edges as before.
5. Take one cut out sleeve and put a marker pin in the centre of the curved (top) edge. Match the marker pin to the shoulder seam (right sides together) and pin. Working from the centre, and pinning outwards, pin the sleeve piece to the sleeve edge of the dress.
6. Stitch in place (pic 3). Repeat for the other sleeve.

7. Try the top on at this stage and measure each sleeve to the required length. Pin, press and sew the hems of both sleeves (see the techniques section on hemming page 23).
8. Pin and sew the side seams.
9. For the neck, with right side facing, start pinning the bias binding at the bottom corner of the front section. Continuing pinning the bias binding until you reach the

shoulder seam. Pin the seam flaps open, make a small fold of the bias binding at the seam (pic 4), and continue pinning the binding until you get to the next seam, make another fold as before and continue pinning right round to the end (see the techniques section on bias binding page 24).

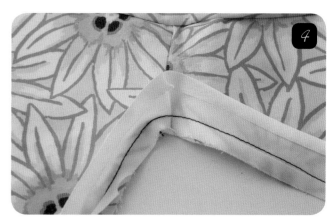

10. Starting at bottom edge of garment, sew along the folded edge of the bias binding all the way round to the other side. Fold over the bias binding, pin and stitch in place making sure you stitch the folds neatly (pic 5). Take out all pins.

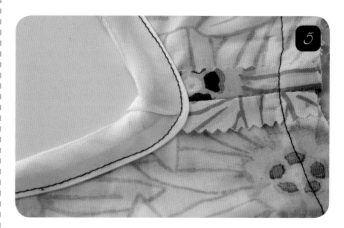

11. Make four ties (see the techniques section on making ties page 28).
12. Place one tie at each corner edge where the top and bottom pieces meet (see main photo). Place one of the other ties on the inside of the garment along the top seam underneath the arm. Place the last tie on the outside of the garment approx 13cm (5in) in from the edge at the same level as the one of the first ties. Try the garment on first to make sure ties are placed correctly for your size before you sewing.
13. Hem the garment to the required length (see the techniques section on hemming page 23).

Cushions can add a splash of colour and comfort to your room and they are very easy to make in any size and use very little fabric. These scatter cushions are made using soft print fabrics with either fluffy velvet backing or the same fabric on both sides. Either bright modern or soft romantic flower prints work brilliantly so choose whichever suits your room best. A zip is inserted so you can remove the covers to wash them, but if you don't feel up to inserting a zip you can hand sew along the fourth edge to close the seam.

Use a 30.5cm (12in) zip on the 40.5cm (16in) cushion. Although it's more difficult to get the cushion pad in, it's easier to sew when you allow for 5cm (2in) at either end.

Techniques used

Hemming (page 23)   Corners (page 24)
How to insert a concealed zip (page 26)

MATERIALS TO BUY
Fabric:
115cm (45in) wide: 50cm (20in) long
150cm (60in): 50cm (20in) long
Cushion pad: 40.5cm (16in) square
Zip: 30.5cm (12in)

CUT SIZES	FINISHED MEASUREMENTS
FABRIC	
(cut two pieces) 44cm × 44cm (17¼in × 17¼in)	41cm × 41cm (16in × 16in)

METHOD

1. Cut two pieces of fabric to size.
2. Put the right sides of the fabric together and measure and pin 1.5cm (⅝in) down along one edge of the fabric in three places for the seam (pic 1).
3. Place the fabric on the ironing board and fold down one side to the line of the pins, press along to make a 1.5cm (⅝in) seam (pic 2).

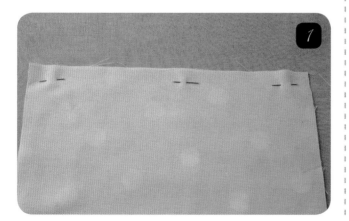

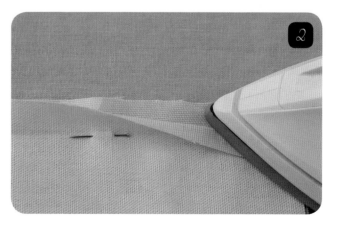

4. Then fold the fabric and repeat on the other side (pic 3).

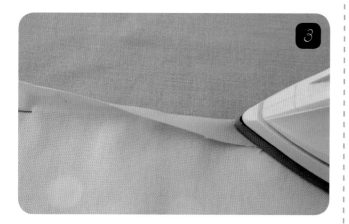

5. Lift up the flaps and tack both sides together along the pressed seam. Remove pins (pic 4).

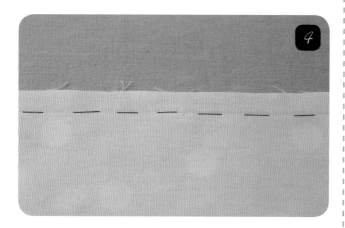

6. Open the seam and press (pic 5).

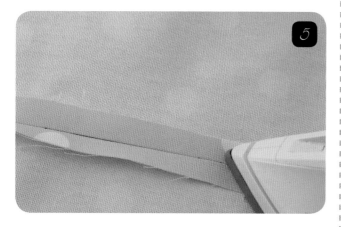

7. Place the zip onto the opened out seam and centralise on the fabric, putting a chalk mark or a pin marker on the fabric at each end of the zip (at the end of the teeth not on its flaps) (pics 6a and 6b).

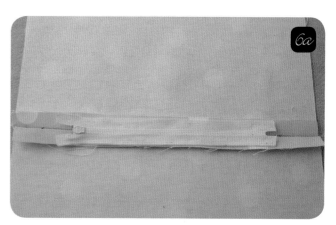

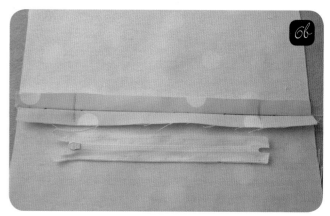

8. Take the zip away from the fabric. Mark the same point on the wrong side of the flaps. With the right sides of the flaps together, sew a short seam at one end of the fabric by lifting up the flaps of the fabric. Sew along the pressed line from the outer edge to approximately 0.6cm (¼in) past the mark. Take the fabric out of the machine, place it at other end and repeat (pic 7).

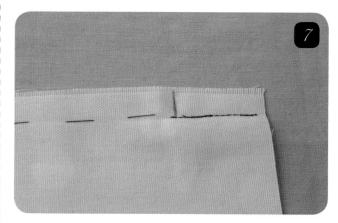

9. Remove any pins before pressing. Take the fabric to the ironing board and with the right sides face down on the ironing board, open seam and press.

10. Place zip, upside down on seam and centralise again.
11. Pin and tack the zip in place on wrong side of fabric (right side of flaps) (pic 8).
12. Remove pins from the fabric.

13. Turn the fabric over and with the right side facing take out the middle seamline tacking stitches for approximately three quarters of the length of the zip at the zip pull end (pic 9).

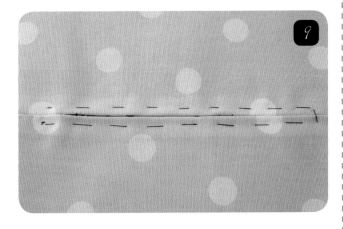

14. Open the zip approximately three quarters of the length (pic 10).

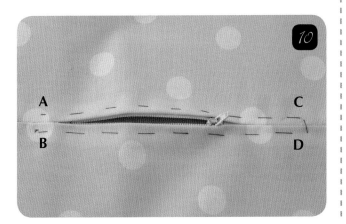

15. Change the foot on the sewing machine for a zipper foot (if you have one, if not just use the standard foot). With right side facing, place the fabric in the machine with the zip horizontal (see point A, pic 10) and sew across at the top of the zip to keep it in place (B). Make sure you avoid the teeth of the zip.
16. Lift the foot, making sure the needle is down, and turn the zip 90 degrees clockwise. Put the foot in the down position and sew up to the zip puller without the foot coming into contact with it. Keeping the needle in the down position, lift up the foot and close the zip. Put the foot down and continue sewing to the end of the zip (C).
17. Leaving the needle in the down position, lift the foot and turn the zip 90 degrees clockwise, place the foot down and sew across to other side of the zip (D), making sure the needle is down when you reach the end.
18. With the needle down, lift the foot and turn the zip 90 degrees clockwise. Open the zip half way, put the foot down and sew to just before the zip pull. With the needle down, lift up the foot, open the zip further and take down past the foot. Put the foot down again and continue sewing to the end of the zip (A). Finish off, cut thread and take out all the remaining tacking stitches. Leave the zip open (see diagram for direction of sewing page 27).
19. Change the foot to the standard foot if necessary. Place right sides of the fabric together, pin then tack a 1.5cm (5/8in) seam around the other three sides of cushion cover. Remove pins.
20. Starting at one side of the cushion cover, sew the seams. Cut the corners diagonally to stop bulking (see the techniques section on corners page 23).
21. Remove all tacking stitches. Open the zip fully. Turn the cushion right side out and insert the cushion pad. (If you have not inserted a zip, insert the cushion pad and hand sew the open seam.)

This easy-to-make dressing gown is a very good garment to start off your sewing career. The pattern includes a simple method of inserting sleeves. Light and comfortable, it looks effective in any type of fabric.

In the photograph we have used dark thread so that you can see the stitches. When sewing your garment match the thread to the colour of the fabric.

Techniques used

Hemming (page 23)   Bias binding (page 24)

MATERIALS TO BUY
Fabric:
115cm (45in) wide: 150cm (59in) long
150cm (60in) wide: 125cm (50in) long
Bias binding: (satin) for edges and belt carriers
2cm wide x 275cm long (^{3}/$_4$in x 108in)

 Template on page 89

METHOD

1. Find your size and cut out the pieces.
2. Pin the back and front pieces at shoulder seams and sew.
3. Open out the sleeve and pin to the opened out shoulder seam, matching the centre of the sleeve to the shoulder seam. Sew.
4. Repeat with the other sleeve.
5. For the belt carriers, don't open the bias binding out, simply fold it in half lengthways and stitch as near to the open edge as possible. Fold the belt carrier in half to make a loop and stitch at the end to hold it in place. Repeat for a second belt carrier.
6. Pin sleeve seam, continuing down side seam, inserting the belt carriers into the seam at waist level. Sew.
7. Put the dressing gown on and pin the sleeve to the required length. Press. Take pins out. Open out fold and cut the edge of the fabric 1cm (^{3}/$_8$in) away from the crease to get rid of excess fabric. Add the bias binding to the sleeve edge (see the techniques section on bias binding page 24).

CUT SIZES	FINISHED MEASUREMENTS
Small	
Back: 92cm long x 60cm wide at bottom (36in x 23^1/$_2$in) **Front:** (cut two) 92cm long x 34.5cm wide at bottom (36in x 13^1/$_2$in)	**Back:** 57cm (22^1/$_2$in) wide at bottom **Front:** 31.5cm (12^1/$_4$in) wide at bottom Hem to length
Medium	
Back: 94cm long x 63cm wide at bottom (37in x 24^3/$_4$in) **Front:** (cut two) 94cm long x 36cm wide at bottom (37in x 14in)	**Back:** 60cm (23^1/$_2$in) wide at bottom **Front:** 33cm (13in) wide at bottom Hem to length
Large	
Back: 96cm long x 67cm wide at bottom (38in x 26^1/$_2$in) **Front:** (cut two) 96cm long x 37.5cm wide at bottom (38in x 14^3/$_4$in)	**Back:** 64cm (25^3/$_4$in) wide at bottom **Front:** 34.5cm (13^1/$_2$in) wide at bottom Hem to length
Sleeves All Sizes	
(cut two) 54cm long x 50cm wide (21^1/$_4$ x 19^3/$_4$in)	52cm long x 47cm wide (20^1/$_2$in x 18^1/$_4$in)
Belt All Sizes	
178cm long x 10cm wide (70in x 4in) Belt carriers (cut two) 12cm (4^3/$_4$in)	175cm long x 4cm wide (69in x 1^1/$_2$in) Belt carriers 12cm (4^3/$_4$in) folded in half

8. Pin the bias binding to the front edges. Sew. Turn over to wrong side, pin and sew.
9. For the belt, fold the shortest edge at each end approximately 1cm (^{3}/$_8$in) and press. Then fold the belt in half lengthways, wrong sides together, and press. Open out the centre and fold both long edges in approximately 1cm (^{3}/$_8$in) and press. Fold the belt in half again lengthways and stitch as near to the open edges as possible.

Give glamour to your bedroom or snuggle up on the sofa in front of the fire with this cosy throw.

Techniques used
Hemming (page 23)   Corners (page 24)

MATERIALS
Fabric:
Vintage floral: 142cm wide x 2m long (56in x 79in)
Snowy Angora Deluxe: 152cm wide x 2m long (60in x 79in) (only width available in this fabric)
Long pins

CUT SIZES	FINISHED MEASUREMENTS
Fabric	
Main fabric: use full width and length of fabric without cutting	142cm wide x 197cm long (56in x 77½in)
Fur fabric: cut to exact size of main fabric	

METHOD
1. Make sure that all the pieces are exactly the same size.
2. Using long pins, pin right sides of both fabrics together. Keep as much of the fur fabric to the inside as possible by pushing the tufts of fur in as you pin (pic 1).
3. Tack, leaving a gap in the middle of the bottom seam of approximately 25cm (10in), so that you can turn the throw through to the right side after sewing.

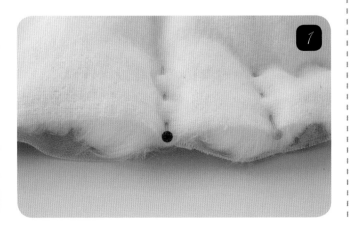

TIP
When cutting fur fabric, cut on wrong side of the fabric, taking small cuts. Try to cut the backing only and not the fur itself and pull the material apart gently.

4. Sew with a straight stitch, 1.5cm (⅝in) from edge, along all four sides, but leaving the gap open. Take out any tacks and pins.
5. Cut the corners diagonally (see the techniques section on corners page 24) (pic 2).

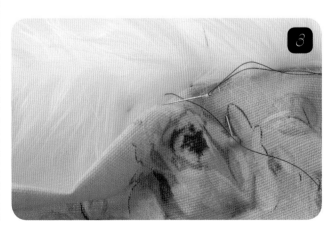

6. Turn the throw through the gap to the right side. Ease out the corners gently using a blunt object such as a knitting needle or chopstick.
7. Hand sew the gap (pic 3). Make sure that your stitches go right through to the backing of the fur fabric.
8. Pick any fur out of the seam using a long pin or a seam picker.

This is a very easy project and you will feel very satisfied with the result whether you are making the bag for yourself or as a gift. The bag is made of felt so it won't fray and there's no need to turn under or finish off the edges. The finished bag has a pretty cotton lining and is just the right size for your make-up and brushes.

Felt is available from most fabric and craft shops and can be bought either by the metre (yard) off a roll, or in ready cut squares.

Techniques used

Hemming (page 23)   Running stitch (page 28)
Appliqué (page 29)

MATERIALS TO BUY

Fabric:

Felt: (buy two pieces) at least 25cm (10in) square
Flower and leaves: 10cm (4in) of each colour
Cotton: (for lining): 46cm x 30cm (18in x 12in)
Zip: 22.9cm (9in)
Thread: Embroidery or standard thread doubled

 Template on page 93

CUT SIZES	FINISHED MEASUREMENTS
Fabric	
Bag and lining: (cut two of each) 23cm x 13.5cm (9in x 5¼in)	20cm x12cm (8in x 4¾in)

METHOD

Template is actual size to be cut out. Follow the tempate to place motif.

1. To make the bag pin the pattern pieces to your fabric and lining and cut out.
2. Pin the appliqué pattern pieces to the fabric and cut out.
3. Place appliqué pieces onto the main fabric, on one side only, and sew in place, using embroidery thread or normal thread doubled and a running stitch (see the techniques section on running stich page 28).

4. Lie the zip, facing upwards, between the pieces of fabric, right side up. With the zip closed, pin the fabric pieces to the zip, ensuring that the end of the zip flaps are lined up with the edge of the fabric. Pin horizontally. Change to a zipper foot if you have one and sew up the sides of the zip (not across the top or bottom edges) (pic 1).

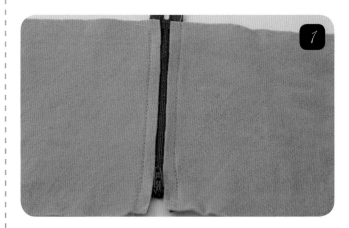

5. With right sides together, starting at the side of the bag where the zip tail ends, pin and sew the side seam 1.5cm (⅝in) from the edge (pic 2).

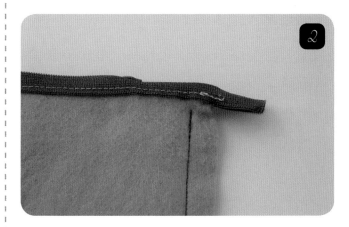

6. Pin and sew the bottom seam. Open the zip 6cm (2½in) so that you'll be able to turn the bag right side out when you've finished sewing, then sew final side seam.
7. Cut the bottom corners of the bag diagonally to stop corners from bulking (see the techniques section on corners page 24) (pic 3).

8. Open the zip fully, turn right side out, tucking the tail of the zip through the gap that has been left. Ease out each corner gently with a blunt instrument such as a knitting needle or a chopstick to ensure that you achieve a nice neat corner.

9. Make a tab for the zip by cutting a small piece of felt, the same width as the zip tail and double the length. Fold it in half and wrap it around the zip tail. Pin and sew in place (pic 4).

10. For the lining, place the pieces of lining right sides together. Pin and sew the seams up two sides and along the bottom.

11. Cut the bottom corners diagonally.

12. With right sides together, fold the top of the lining over and measure against the bag to ensure that the lining will fit just below the zip edges (pic 5). Make larger or smaller to fit as necessary. When you're happy that it's a good fit, press.

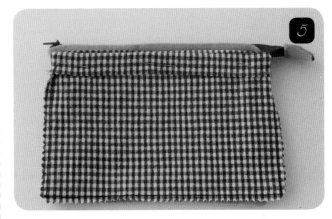

13. Put the lining into the bag and ease it gently in place. Pin and hand sew stitches just over the machine stitches used for securing the zip (pic 6).

Templates

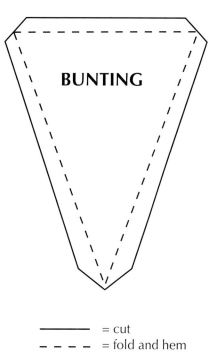

BUNTING

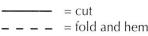
——————— = cut
– – – – – – = fold and hem

KEY

SMALL ———
MEDIUM ———
LARGE ———

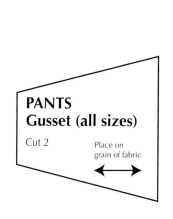

**PANTS
Gusset (all sizes)**

Cut 2

Place on
grain of fabric

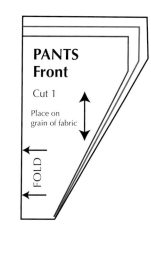

**PANTS
Front**

Cut 1

Place on
grain of fabric

FOLD

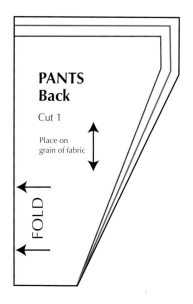

**PANTS
Back**

Cut 1

Place on
grain of fabric

FOLD

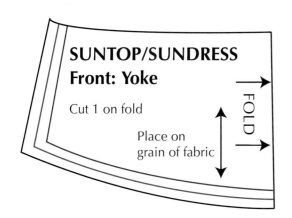

SUNTOP/SUNDRESS
Front: Yoke

Cut 1 on fold

FOLD

Place on
grain of fabric

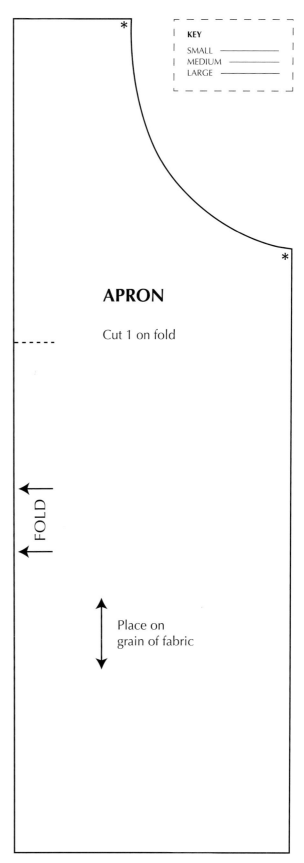

*

*

APRON

Cut 1 on fold

FOLD

Place on
grain of fabric

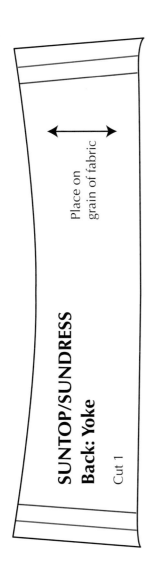

Place on
grain of fabric

SUNTOP/SUNDRESS
Back: Yoke

Cut 1

- - - - Top of pocket   * Attach straps here

36cm (14in)

39.5cm (15½in)

H Attach straps here H

SHOPPING BAG
Main fabric & lining

Not to scale

Cut 4
(main fabric:1 back, 1 front;
lining:1 back, 1 front)

Both ends shaped
like this

SKINNY BELT OR SCARF

Actual Size

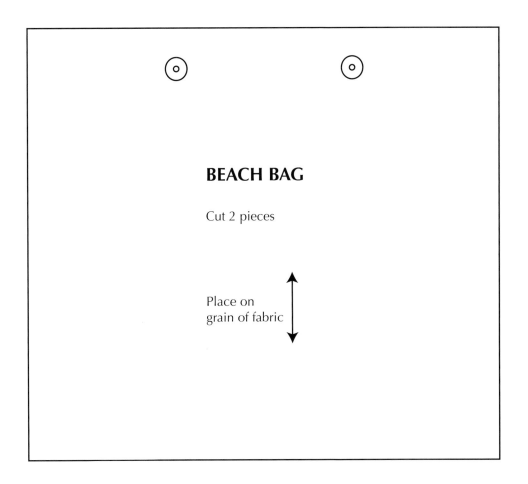

BEACH BAG

Cut 2 pieces

Place on
grain of fabric

eyelet positions

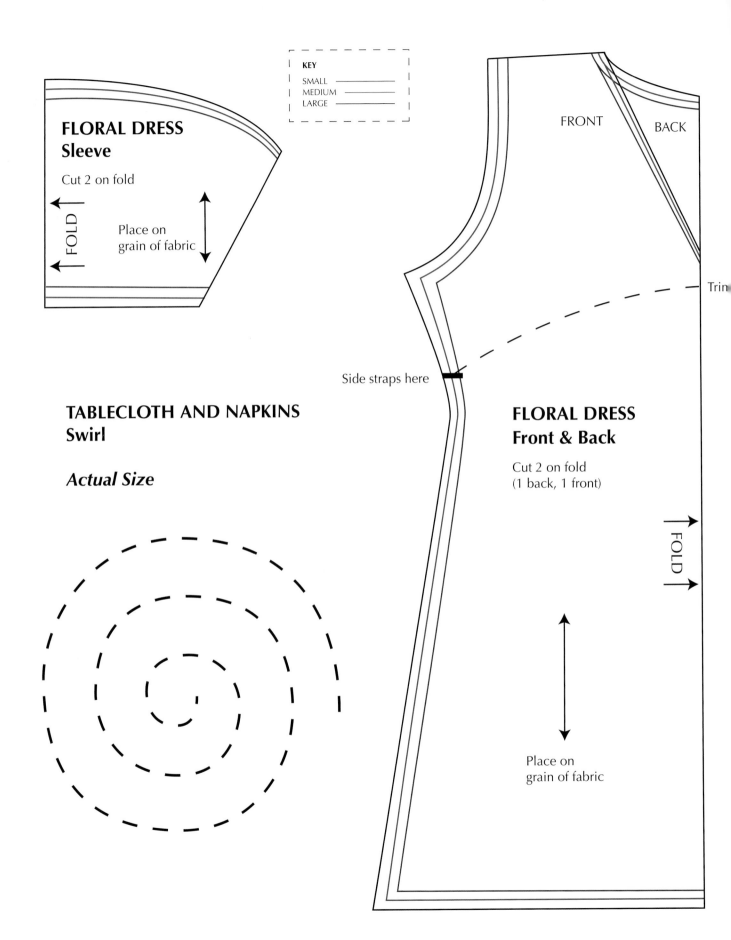

FLORAL DRESS
Sleeve

Cut 2 on fold

FOLD

Place on
grain of fabric

FRONT

BACK

Trim

Side straps here

TABLECLOTH AND NAPKINS
Swirl

Actual Size

FLORAL DRESS
Front & Back

Cut 2 on fold
(1 back, 1 front)

FOLD

Place on
grain of fabric

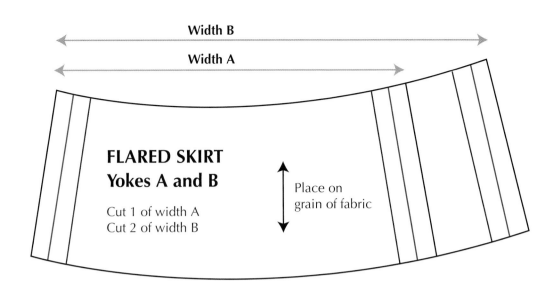

Width B

Width A

FLARED SKIRT
Yokes A and B

Cut 1 of width A
Cut 2 of width B

Place on
grain of fabric

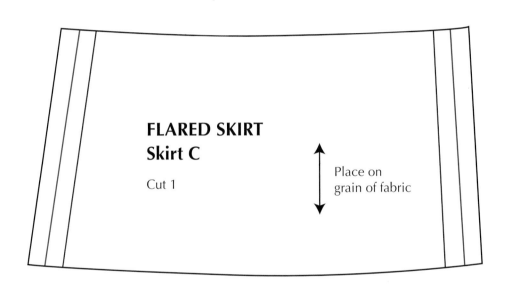

FLARED SKIRT
Skirt C

Cut 1

Place on
grain of fabric

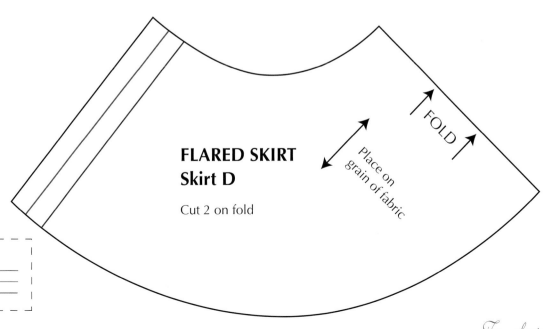

FLARED SKIRT
Skirt D

Cut 2 on fold

Place on
grain of fabric

FOLD

KEY

SMALL

MEDIUM

LARGE

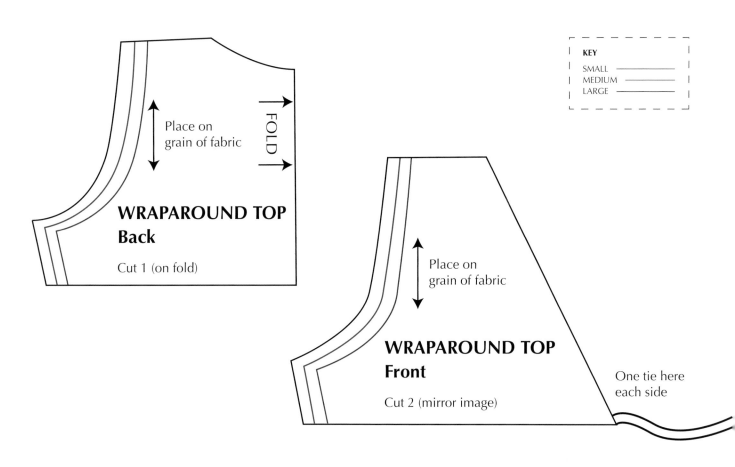

Place on
grain of fabric

FOLD

**WRAPAROUND TOP
Back**

Cut 1 (on fold)

Place on
grain of fabric

**WRAPAROUND TOP
Front**

Cut 2 (mirror image)

One tie here
each side

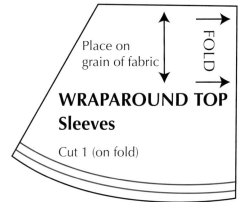

Place on
grain of fabric

FOLD

**WRAPAROUND TOP
Sleeves**

Cut 1 (on fold)

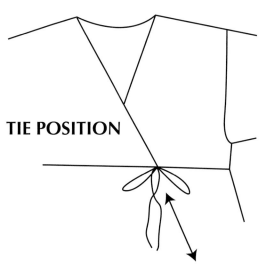

TIE POSITION

Position for the tie

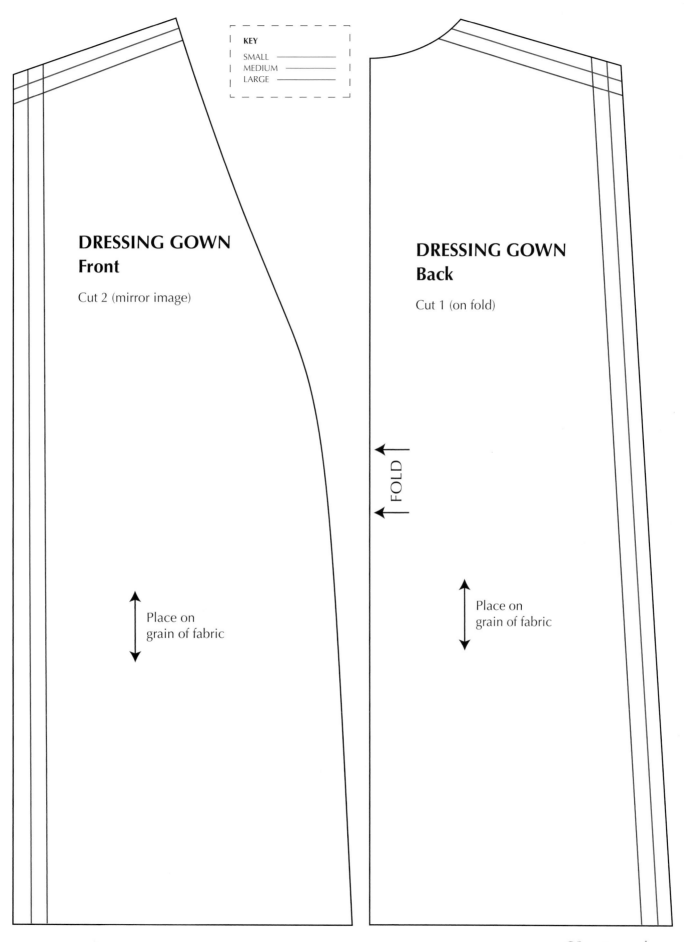

KEY

SMALL ————

MEDIUM ————

LARGE ————

DRESSING GOWN
Front

Cut 2 (mirror image)

Place on
grain of fabric

DRESSING GOWN
Back

Cut 1 (on fold)

FOLD

Place on
grain of fabric

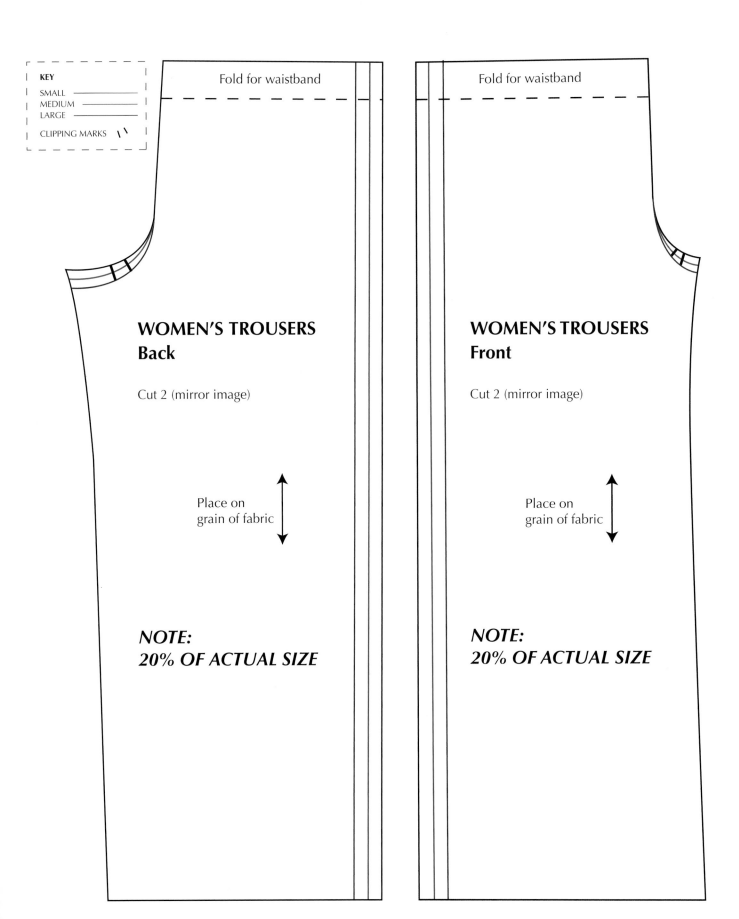

KEY

SMALL ————

MEDIUM ————

LARGE ————

CLIPPING MARKS \ \

Fold for waistband

WOMEN'S TROUSERS
Back

Cut 2 (mirror image)

Place on
grain of fabric

NOTE:
20% OF ACTUAL SIZE

Fold for waistband

WOMEN'S TROUSERS
Front

Cut 2 (mirror image)

Place on
grain of fabric

NOTE:
20% OF ACTUAL SIZE

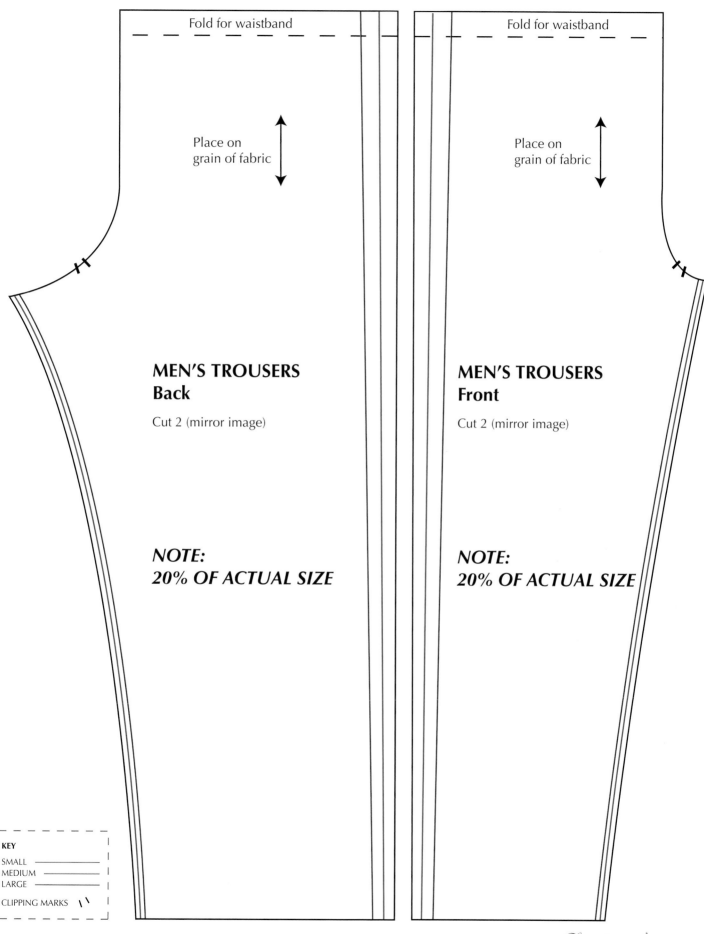

Fold for waistband

Place on
grain of fabric

**MEN'S TROUSERS
Back**

Cut 2 (mirror image)

*NOTE:
20% OF ACTUAL SIZE*

Fold for waistband

Place on
grain of fabric

**MEN'S TROUSERS
Front**

Cut 2 (mirror image)

*NOTE:
20% OF ACTUAL SIZE*

KEY

SMALL
MEDIUM
LARGE

CLIPPING MARKS

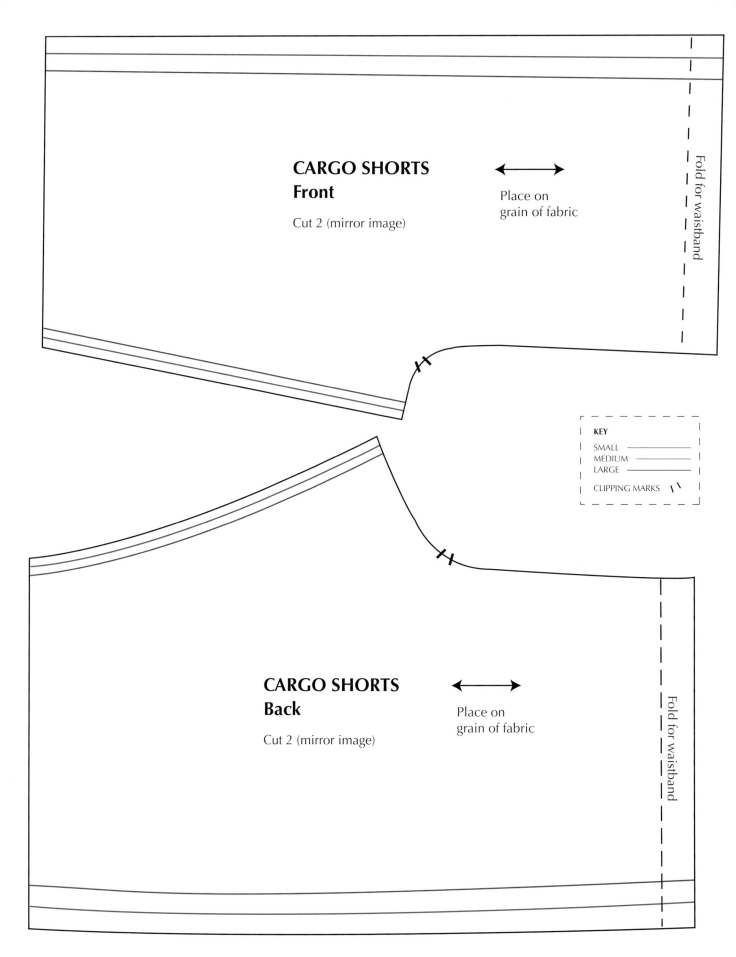

CARGO SHORTS
Front

Cut 2 (mirror image)

Place on
grain of fabric

Fold for waistband

KEY

SMALL
MEDIUM
LARGE

CLIPPING MARKS

CARGO SHORTS
Back

Cut 2 (mirror image)

Place on
grain of fabric

Fold for waistband

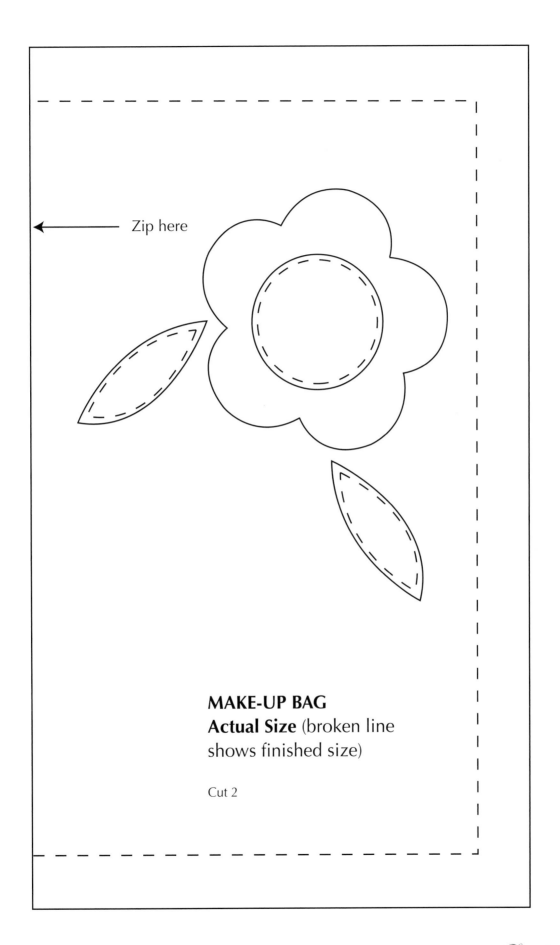

Zip here

MAKE-UP BAG
Actual Size (broken line
shows finished size)

Cut 2

Loose Ends

Resources

The fabrics and equipment for *How To Sew* came from a variety of sources. For many of the projects we used recycled fabrics from old dresses and the handkerchiefs were vintage hand-me-downs. Listed below are the names and addresses of the places we purchased the fabrics and haberdashery for the patterns featured in *How To Sew*. I have also provided contact details for anyone interested in attending a sewing workshop and several essential contacts for anyone wanting further information on sewing.

Laughing Hens
Southover Nurseries
Spring Lane
Burwash
East Sussex TN19 7JB
01435 883777
www.laughinghens.com
sales@laughinghens.com

*Rowan fabrics, Cath Kidston fabrics
and haberdashery
(apron, make-up bag, shopping bag,
sarong and wraparound top)*

John Lewis Partnership
Stores nationwide. Call the customer service line for details of your nearest branch
08456 049049
www.johnlewis.com

*Fabrics and haberdashery
(dressing gown and sundress)*

Liberty's
Regent Street
London W1B 5AH
020 7734 1234
www.liberty.co.uk

*Fabrics and haberdashery
(floral dress)*

Horam Fabrics
Winston House
High Street
Horam
East Sussex TN21 0ER
01435 813306
Fabricshophoram@aol.com

*Fabrics and haberdashery
(cushion cover, throw, clutter cover
curtains and fancy pants)*

Ditto
21 Kensington Gardens
North Laine
Brighton
East Sussex BN1 4AL
01273 603771

*Fabrics and haberdashery
(cargo shorts, women's slouch trousers,
flared skirt, suntop and belt or scarf)*

Deck Chair Stripes
01829 734077
www.deckchairstripes.com

*Specialists in deckchair stripe fabric
(beach bag)*

MacCulloch & Wallis
25-26 Dering Street
London W1S 1AT
020 7629 0311
www.macculloch-wallis.co.uk

*Fabrics and haberdashery
(Fancy pants – green and white gingham
and men's slouch trousers)*

Rosina Fabrics
Mayfield High Street
Mayfield
East Sussex TN20 6AB

*Fabrics, yarns and accessories
(ribbons, zips and threads)*

Fabrics Galore
52–54 Lavender Hill
London SW11 5RH
020 7738 9589
www.fabricsgalore.co.uk

*Fabrics
(cushion cover – circles)*

M. Courts Ltd
31 Commercial Road
London N18 1TP
0208 884 0999
mcourtsltd@btconnect.com

*Wholesale haberdashery supplier
(ribbons, tapes, knicker elastic, threads
and bias binding)*

Sewing Workshops

UK

Laughing Hens
Southover Nurseries
Spring Lane
Burwash
East Sussex TN19 7JB
01435 883777
www.laughinghens.com
sales@laughinghens.com

Artisan Workshops
The Granary
Grange Farm
Ardingly Road
Lindfield
West Sussex RH16 2QY
01444 400183
www.artisan-workshop.co.uk

US

Stitch Lounge
182 Gough Street
(@ Oak in Hayes Valley)
San Francisco
CA 94102-5918
001 415 431 3739
info@stitchlounge.com
www.stitchlounge.com

ACKNOWLEDGEMENTS
This book has been written very much as a team: I am indebted as always to Julian for guiding us along the way, to Roger for keeping a check on my punctuation; to my mother and Christopher for their inspiration and to husband David, Camilla and Maddy for their patience and support; Sian Brown for having the insight to understand and translate the designs into practical diagrams and drawings; the gorgeous models, Maddy, Lydia and Dan. Most of all thanks to Sally Summerfield and Carole McDonald who spent day after day (and some nights) working through all the patterns, photos and methods with vigour and dedication.

Further Sewing Information

UK

ISEW Limited
14 Avondale Road
Waterlooville
Hampshire PO7 7ST
learnmore@isew.co.uk
isew.co.uk
02392 715890

Cath Kidston
8 The People's Hall
2 Olaf Street
London W11 4BE
0207 221 4248
info@cathkidston.co.uk
www.cathkidston.co.uk

Royal School of Needlework
Appt 12A
Hampton Court Palace
East Molesey
Surrey KT8 9AU
020 3166 6932
www.royal-needlework.co.uk
enquiries@royal-needlework.co.uk

Creative Stitches & Hobbycrafts Exhibition
International Craft & Hobby Fair Ltd
Dominic House
Seaton Road
Highcliffe
Dorset BH23 5HW
Exhibitions nationwide. Call the information hotline or see website for details.
01425 272711
www.ichf.co.uk
info@ichf.co.uk

US

Home Sewing Association
PO Box 1312
Monroeville
PA 15146
001 412 372-5950
www.sewing.org